The incredible phenomenon of
CROCKERY COOKERY

First printing: 50,000
Second printing—two weeks later: 200,000
Third printing—three weeks later: 150,000
And still going strong!

Fourteen days after publication, *Crockery Cookery* shot to the top in cooking circles. No wonder. There are about 20 million slow-cooker owners out there who need this book, and their numbers are growing every day! They know this new way of cooking requires *new* recipes—and here they are. *Crockery Cookery* has recipes in abundance for every type of electric crock-type cooker. Mable Hoffman has loaded this great book with tasty, eye-appealing recipes for economy and gourmet meals. She invites you to join the newest cooking craze!

This is the original and authentic
CROCKERY COOKERY
The runaway bestseller by Mable Hoffman

THE AMERICAN HERITAGE COOKBOOK
THE ART OF FISH COOKERY by Milo Milorandovich
THE ART OF FRENCH COOKING by Fernande Garvin
THE ART OF GERMAN COOKING by Betty Wason
THE ART OF ITALIAN COOKING by Mario Lo Pinto
THE ART OF JEWISH COOKING by Jennie Grossinger
BLEND IT SPLENDID: THE NATURAL FOODS
   BLENDER BOOK by Stan and Floss Dworkin
THE COMPLETE BOOK OF MEXICAN COOKING
   by Elisabeth Lambert Ortíz
THE COMPLETE BOOK OF ORIENTAL COOKING
   by Myra Waldo
THE COMPLETE BOOK OF PASTA by Jack Denton Scott
THE COMPLETE BOOK OF WINE COOKERY
   by Myra Waldo
COOKING WITHOUT A GRAIN OF SALT by
   Elma W. Bagg
CROCKERY COOKERY by Mable Hoffman
FANNIE FARMER BOSTON COOKING SCHOOL COOK-
   BOOK by Wilma Lord Perkins
FRENCH CHEF COOKBOOK by Julia Child
THE GRAHAM KERR COOKBOOK by the Galloping
   Gourmet
HORS D'OEUVRE AND CANAPES by James Beard
THE INTERNATIONAL FONDUE COOKBOOK
   by Leonard Louis Levinson
JEANNETTE'S SECRETS OF EVERYDAY GOOD
   COOKING by Jeannette Seaver
MADAME WU'S ART OF CHINESE COOKING
   by Sylvia Wu
THE ONE POT DINNER by Hannah Scheel
THE ROMAGNOLIS' TABLE by Margaret and G. Franco
   Romagnoli
THE SPANISH COOKBOOK by Barbara Norman
THE WALTON FAMILY COOKBOOK by Sylvia Resnick
WHOLE EARTH COOK BOOK by Sharon Cadwallader and
   Judi Ohr
THE WORLD-FAMOUS RATNER'S MEATLESS COOK-
   BOOK by Judith Gethers and Elizabeth Lefft

CROCKERY COOKERY

by Mable Hoffman

BANTAM BOOKS
TORONTO   NEW YORK   LONDON

CROCKERY COOKERY

A Bantam Book / published by arrangement with
H. P. Books

PRINTING HISTORY

H. P. Books edition published February 1975

2nd printing . . . . . March 1975	4th printing . . . . May 1975
3rd printing . . . . . . April 1975	5th printing . . . . June 1975
	6th printing . . . . June 1975

Bantam edition / July 1975

2nd printing . . . . . . July 1975	17th printing . . February 1976
3rd printing . . . . . . July 1975	18th printing . . February 1976
4th printing . . . . . . July 1975	19th printing . . . . March 1976
5th printing . . . . August 1975	20th printing . . . . March 1976
6th printing . . . . August 1975	21st printing . . . . . . May 1976
7th printing . . . . August 1975	22nd printing . . . . . July 1976
8th printing . . September 1975	23rd printing . . . . . July 1976
9th printing . . . October 1975	24th printing . September 1976
10th printing . . . October 1975	25th printing . . November 1976
11th printing . . . October 1975	26th printing . . . January 1977
12th printing . . November 1975	27th printing . . . . March 1977
13th printing . . December 1975	28th printing . . . . March 1977
14th printing . . December 1975	29th printing . . . . . July 1977
15th printing . . December 1975	30th printing . September 1977
16th printing . . February 1976	31st printing . . . . . April 1978

ISBN 0-553-11888-9

Published simultaneously in the United States and Canada

Bantam Books are published by Bantam Books, Inc. Its trade-
mark, consisting of the words "Bantam Books" and the por-
trayal of a bantam, is registered in the United States Patent
Office and in other countries. Marca Registrada. Bantam
Books, Inc., 666 Fifth Avenue, New York, New York 10019.

PRINTED IN THE UNITED STATES OF AMERICA

0 9 8 7 6 5 4 3 2

CONTENTS

INTRODUCTION

Welcome to good eating! Slow cooking is the secret of good cooks the world over. With a modern electric slow-cooking pot, you can enjoy delicious simmered-in flavors of some of the world's best dishes without the time-consuming necessity of constant attention.

You can go to work or spend a day at leisurely shopping while your slow-cooking pot gently mingles flavors and spices—and retains many vitamins high temperatures destroy. You return home to a piping-hot dinner that's ready to serve. It doesn't matter even if you're an hour or two late. It won't burn or taste overcooked. Dinner is ready when you are!

Superb and truly nourishing meals can be prepared with inexpensive meats because slow cooking tenderizes in a special way that broiling or frying just can't duplicate. Meats are juicy and never cooked dry because slow-cookings pots seal in the moisture. Farm-kitchen favorites such as stews and hearty soups simmer to perfection with this new but old way to cook.

Gourmet foods are just as easy with the recipes in this book—such as *Teriyaki Steak, Chicken Marengo, Burgundy Duckling* and *Rhineland Sweet-Sour Cabbage*.

Electric slow-cooking pots are popular because they save time, money and energy. On a low-setting, you'll be cooking with less energy than a 100-watt bulb. You can cook all day for only a few pennies—far less than the cost of cooking the same meal on your kitchen stove. You will also find that the slow-cooking pot does not make your kitchen hot in the summertime.

Gourmet foods, economy and the luxury of time are all yours with this new way of electric slow cooking.

Slow cooking is different and requires special recipes. The recipes in this book were developed specifically for electric slow-cooking pots. Every recipe has been tested and re-tested to bring you success with each meal you prepare. The recipes are arranged in categories: Beef, poultry, vegetables, soups, desserts, etc. Within each group you will find a tantalizing variety so you can plan and serve meals to fit your tastes and preferences.

As you become familiar with this cooking method, you will see how your slow-cooking pot invites culinary creativity. Consider these recipes as basic and add a little pinch of your own ingenuity to the pot.

You'll find slow cooking makes good eating!

MENU PLANNING GUIDE

The most obvious use for your slow-cooking pot is to start a one-pot meal, go to work and return home to a ready-to-serve dinner. But this is just the beginning of slow-cooking convenience! Your slow-cooking pot has eliminated a lot of preparation time. Why not use that extra time to prepare a special dessert or side dish?

Slow-cookers are also convenient for foods which need less than a full day to cook. Whatever your activities, this book has recipes to complement *your* day. Prepare company dinner or a hot lunch, after-game snacks or hearty soups.

Here are a variety of recipes with different cooking times and ideas to adapt your slow-cooking pot to your lifestyle. Which of these situations fits you?

2-4 HOURS COOKING TIME

Invite guests over for the evening or bring home friends from a tennis match or committee meeting. Treat them to some of these piping-hot, slow-cooked specialties. They're sure to be a hit.

> *Hot Buttered Punch*
> *Hot Wine Cranberry Punch*
> *Sloppy Joes or Sloppy Janes*
> *All-American Snack*

3-4 HOURS COOKING TIME

Football and basketball seasons are great times for after-the-game parties. Cold weather and the excitement of a good game contribute to big appetites, so invite your friends over for hot punch and a crunchy snack.

Morning of Game—Mix together all ingredients of *All-American Snack* and cook as directed. Wash slow-cooking pot. One hour before game place ingredients for *Hot Buttered Punch* in slow-cooking pot, start on **LOW**. Spread cooled *All-American Snack* on baking sheet, ready to warm in the oven when you return. Now go and have a good time!

After the Game—Warm snack in 350°F. oven for 15 minutes; serve from nut dishes. Ladle punch into mugs, dot with butter and cinnamon sticks; serve while waiting for snack to heat.

Armchair fans need not miss out on this one—just have everything ready when the game starts.

4-5 HOURS COOKING TIME

Chicken in the freezer? Why not try a new recipe? *Chicken Breasts, Saltimbocca Style* is delicious, and you'll be free to do as you please for the rest of the day.

Night Before—Put chicken breasts out to thaw.
Morning of Dinner—Bone chicken breasts. Follow recipe directions and while chicken is chilling, you can get ready for a day's outing.

Brown chicken and place in slow-cooking pot with other ingredients, turn it on and off you go! If you'll be gone longer than the cooking time, turn the pot on with a timer.

When you come home, add the finishing touches to the chicken and serve with hot rice and applesauce. *Spicy Applesauce* is especially good with chicken. You'll have a dinner sure to please.

4-6 HOURS COOKING TIME

Be everyone's favorite luncheon and party host by serving delightful menus with ease. Don't worry about mid-day entertaining—just serve one of these easy-to-prepare treats:

> *Mock Chili Relleno*
> *Kowloon Chicken*
> *Turkey Loaf*
> *Bishop's Wine*
> *Short-Cut Chili Con Carne*

6-8 HOURS COOKING TIME

You can serve an exquisite company dinner with ease even after shopping or working all day. Just decide what to fix early enough to let meat thaw, start your dinner and be on your way. Supplement elegant main dishes with convenience foods, and you'll serve a memorable dinner with ease and confidence. For starters:

> *Beef Burgundy*
> *Barbecued Spare Ribs*
> *Chicken Breasts, Saltimbocca Style*
> *Chicken Parmigiana*

Here's how to do it with *Teriyaki Steak*. If the meat you have is still frozen, or only partially thawed, don't worry. Frozen meat is easier to cut into thin strips for *Teriyaki Steak*. Place meat and remaining ingredients in slow-cooking pot, set to cook for six hours and enjoy your day.

Round out your dinner menu with frozen Chinese vegetables, instant rice and a green salad with your favorite dressing. Last-minute preparations take only 20 to 25 minutes.

Serve orange sherbet and almond cookies for dessert.

7-8 HOURS COOKING TIME

This elegant company dinner is designed especially for the person who works full-time, yet enjoys entertaining dinner guests during the week. You will need only 15-20 minutes to stuff the chicken and start it cooking, and even less time for last-minute preparation of salad, relish tray and rolls. Your guests will marvel at your organization, and you can serve a dinner to be proud of.

> *Busy Woman's Roast Chicken,*
> served with
> *Salad with Bleu Cheese Dressing*
> *Relish Tray—olives, celery, or*
>   *canned fruits*
> *Rolls and Butter—Refrigerator or*
>   *Brown n' Serve*
> *Coffee-Tea*
> *1-2-3 Jello*
> *Short-Cut Fruitcake (optional)*

Two Days Before—Prepare *Short-Cut Fruitcake.*

Night Before—If chicken is frozen, put out to thaw. Prepare dressing mix, let cool; refrigerate. Peel and cut carrots into 2-inch pieces, ½-inch thick. Place in small amount of water; boil 5 minutes. Drain; cool; refrigerate. Prepare *Jello* as directed, cover dishes with plastic wrap and refrigerate. To prepare *Bleu Cheese Dressing*: Break 4 oz. Danish bleu cheese into small pieces with fork, add 1 pint sour cream, 2 tbs. mayonnaise, and 1½ tsp. lemon pepper seasoning. Mix well and refrigerate.

Approximate preparation time is one hour.

Morning of Dinner—Rinse and dry chicken; season cavity with salt and pepper. Stuff with cold dressing; lightly salt and pepper chicken. Place carrots in bottom of slow-cooking pot. Add stuffed and trussed chicken. Attach timer; set for 7 hours cooking time.

Fifteen minutes before serving, remove chicken from pot, place in roasting pan; brown in 400°F. oven. Prepare salad and relish tray. Heat rolls in oven.

There you have it! A full company dinner with less work than you'd dreamed possible . . . and no worries!

8-10 HOURS COOKING TIME

Now that the do-it-yourself movement is in full swing, why not invite friends over to help with that special painting job? When they're all finished, serve them the best-tasting *Old Fashioned Beef Stew* they've had in years.

Night Before—Cut up and brown meat; drain excess fat; refrigerate. Clean and chop all vegetables, cover with plastic wrap. refrigerate.

That Morning—Place all ingredients in slow-cooking pot, turn on **LOW**, cover and forget it. While dinner cooks, you'll be painting away; your helpers won't have to run to the kitchen to ask what to do next.

Serve something easy for lunch, like instant soup and sandwiches (also prepared the night before).

When the painting is done, make the gravy and set the table while everyone is cleaning up. A sure hit!

8-10 HOURS COOKING TIME

Working people know better than anyone else how hard it is to cook after working all day. You are the people we have written this book for! Start nutritious, taste-tempting meals in the morning, when you're full of energy, then sit down and RELAX when you get home; dinner will be ready! You may find yourself eating better than you have in years by using these energy and time-saving recipes. Here are just a few:

> *Spicy Wine Pot Roast*
> *Gourmet Leg of Lamb*
> *Stuffed Flank Steak*
> *Chinese Style Country Ribs*

Use your imagination to create your own menus. Use similar recipes and cooking times in *Crockery Cookery* to help you adapt your own favorite recipes. Be adventurous; try out your own ideas and substitute ingredients to fit your taste.

Don't limit yourself to recipes that take a certain amount of time. A timer allows you to prepare any recipe. With planning, you can adapt any recipe in this book to your particular needs. And don't hesitate to combine ideas from two recipes to create your own new recipes.

USE & CARE
YOUR SLOW-COOKING POT

An electric slow-cooking pot is a new type of household appliance offering convenience and capability. As with any new appliance, there are some things to learn about its use and care. These are discussed in this chapter.

SLOW COOKING

Low temperature is the success factor in slow cooking. Low heat and long cooking times retain more vitamins and help simmer flavor into food. It is best to use recipe times suggested in this book; however, if you cook longer, don't worry. Your food will not burn because it does not overheat.

LEAVE IT ALONE

The advantage of slow cooking is to *set it and forget it* because there is no need to tend the pot. Don't hesitate to leave your house to do what you want.

Steam and vitamins condense on the
lid and return to the pot to keep food moist and
nutritious even after cooking many hours.

STIRRING

Stirring is not required for recipes in this book or for slow cooking in general. Basting and brushing are needed for some recipes.

KEEP IT COVERED

Leave the lid on. There is no need to keep looking at food as it simmers in a slow-cooking pot. Steam and nutrients are trapped on the lid, condensed and returned to the cooking pot. The steam atmosphere above the food helps cook from the top. Every time you take the lid off, the pot loses steam. After you put the lid back on, it takes 15 to 20 minutes to regain the lost steam and temperature. Thus, taking the lid off means longer cooking times. *Never* remove the lid during the first two hours when *baking* breads or cakes.

COOKING TIMES

Consult the Slow-Cooking Pots chapter for cooking time variations for your particular brand of slow-cooking pot. Until you become familiar with your slow cooker, follow the suggested times. If you prefer softer vegetables or more well-done meat, cook longer than the indicated times.

Generally one hour on **HIGH** is equal to two hours on **LOW**.

HIGH-ALTITUDE COOKING

Allow more time than given in the recipe at high altitudes (over 4,000 feet). Whether you are using a slow-cooking pot, stove, or oven, food takes longer to cook at high altitudes.

Beans take about double the time given in the recipe. To reduce cooking time for beans, cover with water, bring to boil in pan on stove, simmer for two minutes. Let cool one hour. Soak overnight. Return beans to slow cooker and proceed with the recipe.

Baking also requires longer cooking times. See directions on cake mix to adjust for high altitude. Be sure to bake on **HIGH**.

TEMPERATURES

Recipes in this book refer to two temperature settings, **LOW** and **HIGH. LOW** is 200°F (93° C.) and **HIGH** is 300°F (149°C.). Food in the pot seldom gets hotter than 212°F. (100°C.), as discussed on page 29.

MINIMUM LOW TEMPERATURE

Because slow cooking uses very low temperatures, it is important that all food inside the pot is hot enough to cook properly and avoid food spoilage. A minimum safe temperature for food while cooking is 180°F (82°C.). Some adjustable heat controls have low-temperature settings which should not be used for cooking. They are too cool to cook food safely.

BROWNING UNIT

Some recipes refer to slow-cooking with browning units, an extra-high setting of 350°F.-450°F. (175°C.-230°C.) for browning meat quickly before slow cooking. If you brown or heat meat quickly, remember to turn the control knob back to the proper slow-cook setting before leaving the pot unattended. Some slow-cooking pots with this feature include: Corning, Farberware, Nesco, Oster and Regal.

TEMPERATURE SWITCHES

Some slow-cooking pots have a three-position switch, **OFF-LOW-HIGH.** The switch snaps into the desired position as you turn it. You must snap this switch to **LOW** or **HIGH** to cook, not in between.

This switch snaps into the **OFF**, **LOW** or **HI** setting. Do not set the switch between **OFF** and **LOW** or **LOW** and **HI** because the pot will not heat. There are no "in-between" settings.

TEMPERATURE CONTROL UNITS

Other slow-cooking pots have a continuously adjustable thermostatic-heat-control unit to keep the temperature within a few degrees or at the same temperature for hours. The Slow-Cooking Pot chapter gives time and temperature suggestions for your particular brand.

Here is the right way to use a heat-control unit if it is a removable one:

1. Insert the control all the way into the pot.
2. Connect the cord to 120-volt AC outlet.
3. Turn control to desired setting.

To disconnect, turn control to **OFF** and remove the plug from wall outlet. The pot and heat-control housing will be hot after use. If you must remove the heat control before the pot is cool, use a pot holder. Do not touch the metal thermostat probe and do not let the probe come into contact with other materials.

To clean, wipe with a damp cloth. *Do not immerse any electric control unit in water.*

Different heat control
units: Three units
on left, Farberware,
Oster and Sunbeam,
are thermostatically controlled—
you select the desired
temperature. The Crock-Pot
control at right is
a switch with distinct
OFF, LOW or **HI** positions.

PILOT LIGHT

Thermostatic-heat-control units have a pilot light which glows when heating (using electricity) and is off when the pot reaches the desired temperature.

The pilot light turns on and off indicating the temperature is being maintained within a narrow range by switching electricity on and off to the heating unit.

TIMED COOKING

Take complete advantage of the convenience of your slow-cooking pot by using a timer or timed electrical outlet to turn the pot on while you are away.

A timer allows you to prepare recipes that cook in less time than you will be away *and* those you never seem to have enough time to cook—such as squash or roasted chicken. You can have a hot—not burned—dinner when you arrive home.

To use a timer with a slow-cooking pot, *plan for the timer to turn it* ON, *not* OFF. Subtract the recipe cooking time from your expected return time. Set the timer to turn your pot on at this time.

TIMED RECEPTACLE

Many electric ranges have timed receptacles. These are especially convenient but make sure yours works like you think it does before you gamble your dinner on it. To test, plug in an appliance and set the timer to turn on in a short time. Now, turn the appliance ON. If the timed receptacle works, your appliance will start in a few minutes.

TIMERS

If you don't have a timed receptacle, buy an appliance timer. They range in price from $6 to $25. This is the same kind of timer that turns on your house lights to foil burglars while you are away. In addition, you can use it to turn on a variety of appliances, even your coffee pot before you get up in the morning.

The most practical electric timers offer a receptacle for your appliance cord, ON and OFF settings, and wattage ratings high enough for many household appliances. Intermatic, GE and others make the kind you need.

FROZEN FOODS

Frozen foods should be thawed before placing them in your slow cooker. Some glass-lined or metal cooking surface pots (bare-metal, Teflon or porcelainized) can be used with foods which are still frozen. Several extra hours must be added to the cooking time to compensate for the time required for the food to thaw before cooking actually begins. I wouldn't consider doing this with a crockery-lined pot or a crockery pot because I think you'd probably break the crockery.

In some cases, I have recommended using partially thawed (still frosty on the inside) vegetables in stews and soups. This works fine and will not require modifying the times I have given in the recipes.

SPICES

Because little evaporation takes place when cooking with your slow cooker, there are more juices when you finish than you would have with other cooking methods. For this reason you may want to adjust the amount of spices you use in my recipes so they will suit your taste.

FOIL SPEEDS COOKING

You can decrease cooking times a bit by using a piece of aluminum foil on top of the contents or between the lid and the pot. The foil reflects heat back into the food—heat which would otherwise be lost through the lid. This trick can help speed up cooking in a cooker which cooks at lower temperatures than I used for my recipe testing. The temperature charts in the cooker description section show which ones give temperatures which I felt were on the low side of what was needed.

MEAT RACK

A metal meat rack or trivet will keep a roast out of juices and fats in the bottom of the cook pot and prevents the meat from sticking to the bottom. Use a meat rack *only* when the recipes say to; it is not necessary or useful for all meats. It is most useful for fatty meats or roasts which produce a lot of grease while cooking.

This Intermatic timer plugs into a kitchen receptacle. Your appliance plugs in at the bottom.

These Intermatic timers are designed to use with household appliances when you need extra cord length. Model at left has standard **ON-OFF** settings. Multi-program timer at right has tab inserts to turn power **ON** and **OFF** more than once during 24 hours. A great burglar deterrent when used with a lamp.

If you don't have a meat rack, use a trivet. Any style will do. A trivet is often suggested in the Breads and Cakes chapter.

A meat rack is used in some recipes to keep meat out of fatty juices. It is not used or necessary to cook all meats. Use only when directed.

BAKING PANS AND DISHES

You can bake without modifying the recipes in this book in these brands of slow-cooking pots: Corning, Cornwall 4-quart (not tray model), Dominion, Empire, Grandinetti, Hamilton Beach, Penney's, Regal Poly Pot, Reliable Crockery Slow Cooker, Rival, Sears 4-quart (not tray model), Sunbeam, Van Wyck Sim·R· Pot, Wards Crockery Slow Cooker, Wear·Ever Pokey· Pot, West Bend Home Maid Slo-Cooker and Lazy Day Slo-Cooker.

With special care you can also bake in these pots: Farberware, Nesco, Oster, Presto and Regal Pot O' Plenty. These slow-cooking pots are trickier to bake in because they are basically frypans or deep fryers; they heat very quickly and water evaporates more rapidly. Check water once or twice in the middle of baking. If it has evaporated, add more water.

Do not try to bake in the Cornwall tray model or the Sears tray model unless you use water. If all the water evaporates, they will overheat and break. These pots cannot be used dry.

Baking requires a separate pan inside your slow-cooking pot. The Breads and Cakes chapter shows you how to use coffee cans, ring molds, tube pans and soufflé dishes.

Glass lids often get very hot. Use a pot holder to be safe.

Many slow-cooking pots have metal sides that get very hot while cooking. Be careful to avoid touching the hot pot with your hands or arms.

LIDS AND HANDLES

Become familiar with your pot to prevent a burned hand or spill. Lids are glass, plastic or metal. The handle on a glass or metal lid gets hot enough so you'll need a pot holder. Keep the glass handle clean and free of oil so it won't slip out of your grasp.

Pot handles are usually located near the top of the pot. This is the safest location. Handles near the bottom of the pot make the pot unwieldy to handle. Most handles are safe to use but some are dangerously close to the heated exterior surface. Check whether you are going to get burned before you put your hand anywhere on the pot; use pot holders to be safe.

CORDS

Most slow-cooking pots come with a short cord. This is a safety precaution to eliminate long, dangerous dangling cords that can be pulled on by children or tripped over. Many pots have the cord attached which means the cooking pot is non-immersible. You can eliminate some of the nuisance of a dangling cord while washing and handling. Wrap up the cord as short as practical and tie with a rubber band or plastic tie. This helps keep the cord from dangling around the sink and getting wet or in the way.

On pots with attached cords, keep the cord wrapped up with a rubber band or plastic tie. It will be easier to handle, especially when cleaning.

EXTENSION CORDS

Extension cords may be used with most slow-cooking pots if you exercise care. The marked electrical rating of an extension cord should be at least as great as the electrical rating of the appliance—at least 15 amperes. The longer cord should be arranged so that it will not drape over the counter or table top where it can be pulled on by children or tripped over. If the extension cord gets warm or hot, it is not adequate and should not be used.

A SAFE POT

Place your pot on a flat, level surface. Put it where it cannot be accidentally moved, touched or tipped over by guests or children. Place the cord so it cannot be entangled and does not touch the hot surface of the pot.

Some slow-cooking pots are insulated so the outside surface does not get very hot. In this category are the 4½-quart Crock-Pot, Regal Pot O'Plenty and Regal Poly Pot. You can touch these models after a day's cooking and not get burned; even the bottom is only warm. The outside surfaces of some of the other slow-cooking pots will burn you, so be careful. Watch that your children don't try to touch the pot.

BEFORE YOU START COOKING

Wash the inside of your new pot in soapy water. Do not immerse the pot in water unless it has a separate heating unit. Crockery, Teflon, Teflon II, aluminum, porcelain, stainless steel and glass may have a manufacturer's finishing coating you can't see and don't want in your food. Washing removes it.

Teflon, aluminum or stainless steel pots should be seasoned to reduce the chance of sticking and protect the cooking surface. To season your pot, rub the inside surface lightly with cooking oil or shortening. Remove the excess with a paper towel.

Slow-cooking pots with attached cords cannot be immersed. To clean, place pot in empty sink, then fill with warm soapy water. Wash and pour out water. Rinse out inside of pot and dry.

HOW TO CLEAN YOUR SLOW COOKER

Preventive maintenance and care will keep your pot looking new. Don't allow food stains to burn into the finish. Soak the inside of the pot with warm soapy water to loosen food, then scrub lightly with a plastic or nylon pad. Rinse well and dry.

Different brands of slow cookers use different materials. Here are tips on cleaning and caring for the various surfaces.

CROCKERY

Crockery is a term for several varieties of stoneware and earthenware. Slow-cooking crockery pots are fired at high temperatures to make the pot and glazed surface non-porous and safe for cooking. Crockery pots should be washed soon after using. If your crockery liner is removable from the heating unit, it can be dishwasher cleaned or washed as you would any other pot or pan. If the crockery portion is not removable, *do not immerse the entire unit in water.* Fill the pot with hot soapy water to loosen stubborn food.

Use a plastic cleaning pad to remove residue. Do not use abrasive compounds like household cleaners or steel-wool soap pads.

If stains accumulate, remove them with a Teflon cleaner. Use three or four tablespoons of cleaner with enough hot water to cover the stain. Simmer one hour, rinse well and dry.

All crockery can be broken by a sharp blow so use special caution around the sink.

Crockery should not be exposed to *sudden* changes in temperature. Allow the pot to attain room temperature before heating. If the pot is hot, do not fill with cold water.

CAUTION: Do not scrape or scratch crockery to remove stubborn food. Food will stick at the scratch later. Instead, fill the pot with water and let it soak. Also, keep kitchen utensils out of the pot when cleaning up. A knife or handful of silverware can scratch the cooking surface. If the glaze on the cooking surface of the crockery pot should crack, get a new liner or crock. A crack in the glaze can trap food you can never clean out. This could be a place for bacteria to grow and you don't want that!

STAINLESS STEEL

Wash in hot soapy water. Remove food particles with a sponge, vegetable brush and scouring cleanser. You can use a steel-wool scouring pad for any additional cleaning. Do not use steel-wool cleaning pads on the polished outside of your pot. You will scratch the surface, and the mistake is nearly impossible to polish out. Rub the outside of your stainless steel pot with a sponge, cloth or plastic cleaning pad. Rub in the direction of the polishing lines; dry thoroughly to prevent water spots.

If your pot is a stainless steel/aluminum base combination, as the Farberware Pot-Pourri pans, use steel-wool pads to clean up the aluminum on the base.

PORCELAIN AND BAKED ENAMEL

Let pot cool completely before washing. Clean the pot and lid in hot soapy water, using a sponge, dish cloth or plastic pad. A non-abrasive cleaner such as *Bon Ami* may be used if necessary on the porcelain finish. Apply with a cloth or sponge, using a circular motion. DO NOT use a metal scouring pad or harsh scouring powder on the porcelain finish. After washing, rinse pot thoroughly and dry. If detergent is not entirely rinsed off, it can result in stained areas when reheated.

ALUMINUM

Wash pot in hot soapy water. Stubborn food or stains should be soaked and scrubbed off with a plastic or nylon scouring pad. If food is very stubborn, use steel wool pads.

In the event the aluminum cooking surface discolors, follow the stain removal procedure outlined for Teflon, using *Dip It*. Re-season pot after cleaning. Additional usage may cause a white mineral film to form on the cooking surface. Wipe away with vinegar or lemon juice. Re-season pot.

On aluminum slow-cooking pots with a non-stick coating such as the Oster Super Pot, the aluminum base may be cleaned with a commercial degreaser, but be sure not to get the cleaner on the cooking surface. Steel-wool cleaning pads will also help clean up the base.

CORNING WARE & GLASS LINERS

Corning Ware cookware is made of glass-ceramic material which absorbs heat rapidly and holds heat a long time. These qualities make it ideal for slow cooking.

Another special Corning Ware feature is its ability to withstand extreme temperatures and sudden temperature changes. You can take your Corning Ware directly from the freezer or refrigerator and place it on the heating surface.

Corning Ware is very easy to clean; these directions keep it looking and cooking like new.

Usually, you can remove food with hot soapy water and a dish cloth or plastic scouring pad. Do not use metal scouring pads, as these will scratch the ceramic glaze.

For burned-on food, soak pot in soapy water. Use cleanser or baking soda with a damp cloth.

When sugary or starchy foods stick to Corning Ware, soak or boil with baking soda (3 tbs. soda to 1 qt. water). For greasy foods, soak pot in ammonia and water. Use cleanser if necessary.

TEFLON AND TEFLON II

Wash with warm soapy water and dry thoroughly. Teflon is damaged by steel-wool scouring pads or abrasive kitchen cleansers. A plastic cleaning pad (nylon) can be used on stubborn food.

In time, a Teflon surface will discolor over the heating element. This is normal and will not affect Teflon anti-stick and easy-clean qualities. To reduce discoloration, thoroughly wash your pot after each use. When discoloration becomes noticeable, you can remove it with special appliance stain removers like *Dip It,* available at your grocery store. Follow the manufacturer's instructions and wear gloves. Wipe off any remover that gets on the outside of your pot or pan; the solution may remove the baked enamel or porcelain finish. After removing stains, rinse thoroughly and dry. Re-season your pot by rubbing lightly with cooking oil.

CAUTION: Do not scrape or scratch Teflon or non-stick finish to remove stubborn food. Food will stick at the scratch later. Instead set the pot to soak. Also, as good practice, keep your kitchen utensils out of the pot when cleaning up. A knife or handful of silverware can scratch the cooking surface.

Teflon II is now available in some pots. DuPont has improved the finish to last longer, clean easier and stain less.

METRIC CONVERSION CHART

Metric Units:

1 kilogram (kg)	= 1000 grams
1 gram (gm)	= 1000 milligrams
1 milligram (mg)	= 1000 micrograms (mcg)

Weight:

Metric			*U.S. Avoirdupois*
1 kilogram =	1000	gm	= 2.2 pounds
0.1 kilogram =	100	gm	= 3.52 ounces
0.454 kilogram =	454	gm	= 1.0 pound
0.028 kilogram =	28.4	gm	= 1.0 ounce

Volume, Liquid:

3.785 liters			= 1 gallon
1.000 liter =	1000	ml	= 1.06 quarts
0.946 liter =	946	ml	= 1 quart
0.473 liter =	473	ml	= 1 pint
0.227 liter =	227	ml	= 1 cup
0.014 liter =	14.2	ml	= 1 tablespoon
	4.7	ml	= 1 teaspoon

Weight per Volume of Water:

1 liter =	1 kg	
1 milliliter =	1 gm	= 1 cubic centimeter
1 quart =	946 gm	
1 cup =	227 gm	= 8 ounces

TABLE OF MEASUREMENTS

3 teaspoons	=	1 tablespoon
16 tablespoons	=	1 cup
2 cups	=	1 pint
2 pints	=	1 quart
4 quarts	=	1 gallon
8 fluid ounces	=	1 cup
1 fluid ounce	=	2 tablespoons
16 ounces	=	1 pound
4 tablespoons	=	¼ cup
8 tablespoons	=	½ cup
dash	=	less than ⅛ teaspoon

CONSUMER'S GUIDE TO SLOW-COOKING POTS

There is a particular slow-cooking pot to suit your needs. Some are designed solely for slow cooking—others are also frypans or deep fryers. Your choice of a slow-cooking pot will depend on the appliances you already have and use, and the size recipes you prepare.

Each brand has different capacity, shape, cooking surface, outside finish, handles, cord and temperature settings.

This chapter tells you things you need to know about each slow cooker, such as special handling hints so you don't get burned. Here are instructions for temperature control settings and times to match recipes in this book for each cooker. Special temperature charts show how each pot heats. And, there are clean-up hints, too!

These manufacturers have registered trademarks and product names referred to in *Crockery Cookery*.

Corning Electromatic
Corning Ware
Cornwall Crockery Cooker
Dobie
Dominion Crock-A-Dial & Crock-A-Dial II
DuPont Teflon and Teflon II
Empire Easy Meal
Farberware Pot-Pourri
General Electric Lexan
Grandinetti All American Crockery Casserole
Grandinetti All American Crockery Cook Pot
Hamilton Beach Continental Cooker, Crock-Watcher, Simmer-On
Intermatic Time-All
K-Mart LaCuisine Sim·R·Pot
Nesco Pot Luck
Oster Super Pot

Penney's Slow Cooker/Fryer
Penney's Slow Crockery Cooker
Presto Slow Cookers
Regal Mardi Gras Pot O'Plenty
Regal Poly Pot
Reliable Crockery Slow Cooker
Rival Crock-Pot
Robeson Sim·R·Pot
Scotch-Brite
Sears/Simpson Crockery Cooker
Sunbeam Crocker Cooker Fryer & Crocker Frypan
Van Wyck Sim·R·Ware
Van Wyck Sim·R·Pot
Wards Crockery Slow Cooker
Wear·Ever Pokey·Pot
West Bend Colonial Crock Slo-Cooker
West Bend Home Maid Slo-Cooker
West Bend Lazy Day Slo-Cooker

Co-author Howard Fisher made the temperature tests. Heating was measured at each of the control settings. Manufacturers do change specifications from time to time—and not all pots of the same model are identical. Your pot may cook slower or faster than we say it will in the Temperature & Recipe Times descriptions. Your pot will probably perform very closely to the temperatures shown.

HOW TO READ TEMPERATURE CHARTS

The wide grey bands in each chart represent the recipe **HIGH** and **LOW** temperature curves for comparison with all pots.

Black lines show the temperatures attained at each pot setting shown. Note the temperature lines for many pots exceed 300°F. *Food actually never gets this hot in your pot.* Cooking oil was used in one pot of each type to measure temperatures beyond the boiling point of water so you could see the relative heating characteristics for all the pots we tested.

A normal cooking mixture of meat, vegetables and liquid does not heat more than a few degrees above the boiling point of water (212°F. or 100°C.). Steam generated from the hot water condenses on the lid and drips down the sides of the crock to cool the pot and cooking mixture while maintaining a near-boiling temperature. Oil does not provide this cooling action, so our charts show higher temperatures.

Pot capacities are important when considering the relative temperatures of two pots. For instance, the 5½-quart Reliable or 5½-quart Wards and 8-quart Cornwall are designed to cook large quantities of food. Their higher wattage brings a large amount of ingredients to the proper cooking temperature and holds the temperature. To use our recipes with one of the large-capacity pots, reduce recipe times or double the recipe quantities. Then the recipe times and temperature settings will work fine.

2½ quart

Corning Table Range Temperatures

350° F. SETTING

240° F. SETTING

Corning Electromatic Table Range

You can slow cook with this unit. A separate Corning Ware casserole holds the food and rests on the Corning Ware cooking surface. The cord is detachable.

Temperature & Recipe Times—The variable temperature control has settings from 200°F. to 500°F. For the recipes in this book, set the temperature to 240°F. for LOW and 350°F. for HIGH. Use times provided in the recipes.

Cleaning—Do not immerse heating unit in water. Clean cooking surface with baking soda or other mild cleaner. Wipe wood grain and metal trim with a sudsy paper towel. The Use and Care chapter tells how to clean Corning Ware.

2½-quart Casserole—Usable capacity is 1¾ quarts.

4½-quart Dutch Oven & Rack—Usable capacity of this casserole is 3½ quarts.

Cornwall 4-quart Crockery Cooker

Usable capacity is 3½ quarts. This crockery pot has a painted-metal outside finish with attached cord. This lid is glass. The outside of the pot and the lid get very hot so use a pot holder to remove the lid and pick up the pot only by the handles. This cooker heats from the sides to provide even heat distribution from top to bottom.

Temperature & Recipe Times—The temperature switch has two positions: MED and HI. For recipes in this book MED should be used whenever LOW is called for. Use HI for HIGH settings. Use the times provided in the recipes.

Cleaning—Do not immerse to clean. Fill empty pot with water to soak off stubborn food. Use and Care chapter tells how to clean crockery. Wipe off outside of cooker with a damp cloth.

2½ quart

Cornwall 2 1/2-qt. Temperature (tray model)

Cornwall Tray Model Crockery Cookers

These cookers differ from the previously discussed self-contained units in that they have an electric heating base and a separate crockery pot with lid. Each size allows you to cook a different quantity of food. The painted rectangular heating base has wooden handles at each end. There is an attached cord. The pot sits in a shallow heating well in the center of the heating base.

The crockery pots are dishwasher and oven safe, but you should not place the pot on any stove burner because that will probably break the pot. Always put ingredients into the pot *before* placing it on the heating base. If the crockery has been in the refrigerator, allow it to warm up to room temperature before placing it on the heating base. Turn on the heating base only after the crockery pot with its contents has been placed in the heating well.

WARNING: There must be at least one cup of liquid in any recipe used in this pot. Do not let the pot operate dry for baking and do not let all of the liquid evaporate. This pot will overheat and probably break if the liquid is allowed to evaporate.

The heating base may be used to warm other pots and pans for keeping food warm, but do not use the base as a griddle. Because both the pot and the heating base become very hot, use a pot holder or mitts to remove the pot. Lift it only by the handles. Do not attempt to move the base without pot holders. There are wooden ends, but these offer little protection against getting burned by the hot heating

4½ quart

Cornwall Tray Model Crockery Cookers

base. The heating bases smoke at first because the protective coatings are burned off as the heating element warms up.

Temperature & Recipe Times—Set the 4½- and 8-qt. temperature controls to 2 for LOW and 3 for HIGH to use with recipes in this book. Position 1 is too cool to cook food properly. It is only designed for warming. Use the times given in the recipes. See special temperature note for 2½-quart model below.

Cleaning—Never immerse the heating base in water. Wipe it clean with a damp cloth after it is completely cool. The Use and Care chapter explains how to clean crockery.

2½-quart—Usable capacity 2 quarts. This pot is suited for one or two people. For the 4 to 6 serving recipes in this book, use one-half the ingredients. Setting 3 on the temperature control is equal to LOW. Use those recipes which cook only on LOW because this pot will not attain a temperature equal to a HIGH setting on other pots.

4½-quart—Usable capacity 3 quarts. Recipes serving 4 to 6 fit nicely.

8 quart

Cornwall Tray Model Crockery Cookers

8-quart—Usable capacity 7 quarts. Great for family-size or party meals. Double 4 to 6 serving recipes to take advantage of the capacity. If you do not double small recipe quantities, reduce cooking times.

Dominion Crock-A-Dial & Crock-A-Dial II

Usable capacity of these pots is 3 quarts. The liner in the *Crock-A-Dial* is crockery. *Crock-A-Dial II* has a glass liner. Sides are painted metal and the lids are glass. Cords are attached. Both units have heating coils around the liner to provide even top-to-bottom heating. The outside of the pot gets very hot. Use pot holders or mitts to remove the lid and pick up the pot only by the handles.

Temperature & Recipe Times—LOW COOK and HIGH COOK settings are somewhat lower than called for in the recipes and may require slightly longer cooking times. The *Crock-A-Dial* has an added AUTO-SHIFT setting which cooks for the first two hours at the high end of the LOW COOK setting, then switches to the LOW COOK setting. With AUTO-SHIFT, recipes calling for cooking on LOW should cook perfectly at the times specified in the recipes.

Cleaning—Do not immerse these pots. Wipe off the outside with a damp cloth. The Use and Care chapter tells how to clean crockery and glass.

Empire Easy Meal Slow Cooker

Usable capacity 2½ quarts. This small-capacity slow cooker has a removable aluminum cooking well. The heating pot and lid are painted aluminum. The outside of the pot gets very hot, so use hot pads or mitts and always pick up the pot by the handles. The temperature control is close to hot metal. Be careful to avoid burning yourself. Food should only be placed in the removable cooking well insert.

Temperature & Recipe Times—The variable temperature dial does not have an OFF position. Unplug the detachable cord to turn the pot OFF. The HI setting heats very slowly, then gets very hot. LO is too low for slow cooking. For recipes in this book, set the temperature to MEDIUM for LOW. Use a one o'clock position for HIGH. This unit does not cook food as evenly as crockery-lined pots because the thin-walled aluminum cooking well does not heat uniformly. Cooking a small roast requires turning it over so it will cook evenly. Other foods may require occasional stirring. Use the recipe times provided.

Cleaning—The aluminum pot stains easily, but is easy to clean with *Dip It*. The heating pot is not immersible and should be cleaned with a damp cloth after the pot is unplugged and cool.

5 quart

Farberware 3- and 5-qt. Temperatures

300° F. SETTING

200° F. SETTING

Farberware 3- and 5-quart Pot-Pourri

Usable capacity 2½ and 4 quarts. These stainless-steel, all-purpose cookers are good for slow cooking, regular cooking and deep frying. The 5-quart model's high-domed lid allows extra height for cooking chickens or larger cuts of meat. The 3-qt. model has a long handle for one-hand carrying, but use both hands because a full pot is heavy. Carry these pots with the handles because all of the metal gets hot. The cord detaches with the temperature-control unit. Handy hint to prevent boil-overs: Fill the pot only ⅔ full of liquid.

Temperature & Recipe Times—Set the control at 200°F. for LOW and 300°F. for HIGH to fit the recipes. These pans attain selected temperatures within only a few minutes, so cooking times are shorter than given by the recipes. An 8 to 10 hour recipe should be reduced to a total time of 6 to 8 hours. Recipes with shorter times should be reduced by ¼ to ½ of the recommended time.

Cleaning—These pots can be immersed for cleaning. The Use and Care chapter explains how to clean stainless steel. Do not immerse the temperature control unit. Wipe it clean with a damp cloth when it is cool.

Grandinetti 4-qt. Temperatures

HI

LOW WITH FOIL

LOW

Grandinetti 4-quart All American Crockery Casserole

Usable capacity $3\frac{1}{2}$ quarts. The removable crockery casserole is an attractive serving dish which can be used at your dinner table. It is oven-proof and dishwasher safe, but you should not place the casserole on a stove burner or electric element because this will break the crockery. Do not turn pot ON before inserting casserole or you may break it. Lexan case and lid stay cool. The cord is attached. When you store food in the pot, allow the crockery to warm up to room temperature before re-heating or the bowl may break. To hasten warming, place the pot in warm—not hot—water.

The separate heating case heats evenly from the sides and should be used only to heat the casserole.

Temperature & Recipe Times—Make sure to turn the heat control switch to LOW or HIGH exactly. This pot cooks slower than the $3\frac{1}{2}$ and 5-quart Grandinetti models. Increase the maximum recipe times by at least two hours. Meat recipes requiring five hours or longer must be cooked at least an additional four hours on LOW, or two hours more on HIGH. If your food does not stand taller than the casserole lip, match recipe LOW times exactly by placing a piece of foil across the pot. Then replace the lid. This decreases the cooling atmosphere and speeds cooking. Do not use this method on HIGH.

Cleaning—The casserole can be put in the dishwasher. See the Use and Care chapter for details on cleaning crockery. Separate heating unit is not immersible. Wipe it off with a damp cloth if it becomes dirty.

Grandinetti 3½-quart All American Crockery Cook Pot

Usable capacity 3 quarts. This popular pot fits most 4-5 serving recipes well. The pot has a painted-metal outside surface with a crockery liner and glass lid. The cord is attached. Do not touch the outside metal surface because it gets very hot. Plastic handles are on the sides. Hold onto them firmly. Heating elements wrapped around the pot provide even heating.

Temperature & Recipe Times—Make sure to turn the heat control switch to LOW or HIGH exactly. Use times provided in the recipes.

Cleaning—Because this pot is not immersible, fill it with warm soapy water to soak off stubborn food. Wipe off the outside with a damp cloth. The Use and Care chapter tells how to clean crockery.

5 quart

Grandinetti 5-qt. Temperatures

Grandinetti 5-quart All American Crockery Cook Pot

Usable capacity 4 quarts. This practical wide-mouth pot is ideal for roasts, chicken and large meals. Detachable cord includes temperature control. This pot has a painted-metal outside surface with a crockery liner. Do not touch the outside metal surface because it gets very hot. Lid stays cool because it is Lexan. Grasp the plastic handles on the sides firmly because they are slippery and sometimes hard to hold onto. Heating elements wrapped around the pot provide even heating of the contents.

Temperature & Recipe Times—Make sure the heating control switch is turned exactly to LOW or HIGH. The heat control unit must be pushed all the way into the pot. Turn OFF when inserting or removing the control unit. Use times provided in the recipes.

Cleaning—This pot is not immersible. Fill the empty pot with warm soapy water to soak off stubborn food. Wipe off the outside with a damp cloth. The Use and Care chapter tells how to clean crockery.

Hamilton Beach Continental Cooker, Crock-Watcher and Simmer-On

Usable capacity of these pots is 3 quarts. Liners for the *Crock-Watcher* and *Simmer-On* are crockery. *Continental Cooker* and *Simmer-On II* are glass-lined. Sides are painted metal and the lids are glass. Cords are attached. All models have heating coils around the liner to provide even top-to-bottom heating. The outside of the pots get very hot. Use pot holders or mitts to remove the lid and pick up the pot only by the handles.

Temperature & Recipe Times—HIGH COOK and LOW COOK settings are somewhat lower than called for in the recipes and may require an added 2 hours or more on many recipes. The *Continental Cooker* and *Crock-Watcher* have an added AUTOSHIFT setting which cooks for the first two hours at the high end of the LOW COOK setting, then switches to the LOW COOK setting. With AUTO-SHIFT, recipes calling for cooking on LOW should cook perfectly at the times specified in the recipes.

Cleaning—Do not immerse these pots. Wipe off the outside with a damp cloth. The Use and Care chapter tells how to clean crockery and glass.

Nesco Pot Luck Cooker

Usable capacity $4\frac{1}{2}$ quarts. This cooker is fine for large meals and poultry. The painted all-metal pot has a removable metal liner with a porcelain-enamel cooking surface. It comes with a detachable cord and a meat rack. While this pot is sold as a slow-cooking unit, it is really a roaster with an added low-temperature setting. The high temperature range reaches 500°F. The primary item that separates this model from other slow cookers is two steam holes in the lid. These lose steam and liquid when used for slow cooking. If you intend to use one of these primarily for slow cooking, I suggest you close the lid holes with epoxy to avoid having to add more liquid at the start or while cooking so food does not dry out. The outside surface gets very hot and you must handle the unit by the handles and preferably with hot pads. Wraparound heating elements provide even heat from top to bottom.

Temperature & Recipe Times—Use the 200°F. LOW position for LOW. Use a 250°F. setting for HIGH. DO NOT USE THE 300°F. SETTING WITH THESE RECIPES. On an 8 to 10 hour recipe you must reduce cooking time to 6 to 8 hours. For shorter times, reduce time by $\frac{1}{4}$ to $\frac{1}{2}$.

Cleaning—The removable porcelain-enameled liner cleans easily with hot soapy water in the sink or dishwasher. Do not immerse the heating unit in water. Wipe it clean with a damp cloth.

Oster Temperatures

300° F. SETTING

200° F. SETTING

Oster 8-quart Super Pot

Usable capacity 7 quarts. This versatile cooker/fryer has a wide temperature range and large capacity. It can be used for warming and serving, slow cooking, steaming, canning and deep frying. The deep pot will hold large roasts, chickens, and even a tube pan for baking. A trivet is included. The black Fluon non-stick cooking surface is similar to Teflon. The aluminum pot has a porcelain outer finish. The long, narrow handles are positioned so you can burn your hands unless you carefully place a pot holder between each hand and the outer surfaces of the pot. This pot is heavy when filled and you should cook and serve from it without moving the pot whenever possible. The cord is detachable.

Temperature & Recipe Times—This pot is also a deep fryer so it reaches selected temperatures in about 5 minutes— much quicker than crockery-lined pots. Recipe times must be reduced to avoid overcooking. On 8 to 10 hour recipes, reduce cooking time to 6 to 8 hours. For shorter times, reduce total time by $\frac{1}{4}$ to $\frac{1}{2}$. Set the temperature control to 200°F. for LOW and 300°F. for HIGH. Recipes in this book may be doubled to take full advantage of the size of this big pot.

Cleaning—This pot is especially convenient to clean because it is immersible. Oster recommends keeping it out of the dishwasher so the cooking surface will last longer.

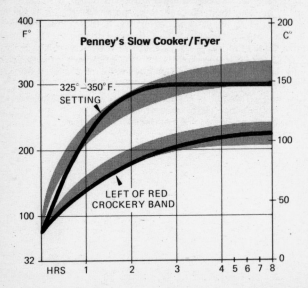

Penney's Slow Cooker/Fryer

325° – 350° F. SETTING

LEFT OF RED CROCKERY BAND

Penneys Slow Cooker/Fryer

Usable capacity 4 quarts. This unit cooks slowly and includes a removable crockery pot. The heavy-wall crock provides even heat distribution, even though heating is only from the bottom. A large lip on the pot makes it easy to handle and it is dishwasher safe and oven proof. This unit is both a cooker and a fryer, with high temperatures for deep frying. The cooker/fryer cooking surface is Teflon-coated.

Temperature & Recipe Times—For the recipes in this book, use 200°F. for LOW. Because there is no 200°F. marker on the dial, set it just to the left of the red CROCKERY band. For HIGH, set the dial between 325°F. and 350°F. Cooking times in the recipes work fine with this pot.

Cleaning—Remove the empty pot and fill with warm water to soak off stubborn food. The slow cooker/fryer heating portion does not get very dirty with slow cooking. Wiping with a damp cloth will usually clean off any spilled food. Do not immerse the cooker/fryer unit.

Penneys Slow-Crockery Cooker

Usable capacity 3 quarts. Most 4-5 serving recipes fit this pot well. This pot has a crockery liner, glass lid and the cord is attached. Wraparound heating elements provide even cooking. The painted metal outside surface and lid get very hot and you should use hot pads and caution in handling them.

Temperature & Recipe Times—Temperature settings of LOW and HIGH are exactly as found in the recipes. Cooking times are the same as provided in the recipes. Turn the knob exactly to LOW or HIGH or the pot will not heat.

Cleaning—This pot is not immersible. Fill the empty pot with warm soapy water to soak off stubborn food. Follow the Use and Care chapter recommendations for cleaning crockery.

5 quart

Presto Temperatures

2 3/4 & 5-QT. (SET BETWEEN HI & BROWN)

5-QT. HI

2 3/4-QT. HI

Presto 2¾- and 5-quart Slow Cookers, Presto Create 'n Serve Pan, Presto Deep Fryer, and Sears Create 'n Serve Pan

Usable capacities are 2 quarts for all of the 2¾-qt. models, and 4 quarts for the 5-qt. slow cooker and deep fryer. These units have a non-stick cooking surface similar to Teflon. The lids are glass on the slow cookers and painted aluminum on the Create 'n Serve Pans and Deep Fryers. The 5-qt. models are the same unit with several additional inches of depth. These pots stand solidly and the handles are conveniently at the top of the pot. The glass lid gets hot and it also tends to slide when you move the pot, so be careful with it. The temperature control is part of the detachable cord.

Temperature & Recipe Times—Use the HIGH setting when recipes in this book say LOW. HIGH on this book is between HI and BROWN, with OFF at an 8 o'clock position. These pots reach selected temperature fast—usually in about 5 minutes. This is so much quicker than crockery-lined pots that the cooking times for recipes in this book must be reduced. On an 8 to 10 hour recipe, reduce cooking time to 6 to 8 hours. For shorter times, reduce the total time by ¼ to ½.

Cleaning—These cookers are immersible and easily cleaned. Follow the Use and Care chapter recommendations for cleaning Teflon.

Regal Mardi Gras Pot O'Plenty

Usable capacity 4 quarts. This combination cooker/fryer uses Teflon II on the cooking surface. The outside finish is a scratch-resistant material called Lexan. The lid is metal. The plastic outer case insulates the pot and you can safely handle it after a day's cooking. Heating elements are on the bottom. This is not a "set it and forget it" pot—you must watch your food while using it—at least until you have learned how to use the temperature settings and cooking times. Hot spots at the bottom of the pot can burn your food so you should plan to turn meats and stir occasionally to avoid scorching.

Temperature & Recipe Times—The temperature control lever is continuously variable with indications 1 to 8. There is considerable "play" in the lever and any setting you choose is only an approximation. To use recipes in this book set at 2 for LOW and 3 for HIGH. This pot heats quicker than crockery-lined pots and cooking times must be reduced accordingly. For 8 to 10 hour recipes try cooking times of 6 to 8 hours. For shorter recipe times, reduce the total time by $\frac{1}{4}$ to $\frac{1}{2}$.

Cleaning—Do not immerse this pot. Fill it with warm water to soak off stubborn food. Teflon II makes the pot easy to clean. The Use and Care chapter tells how to clean Teflon II.

Regal Poly Pot

Usable capacity 5 quarts. This large cooker has white Teflon II on the aluminum cooking surface. A glass lid covers the wide-mouthed pot. The scratch-resistant Lexan outer case insulates the pot and you can safely handle the case after a day's cooking. A short cord is attached.

Temperature & Recipe Times—There is no manual temperature setting on this pot. The pot is ON when plugged in. To turn it OFF, unplug the cord. An automatic heat control cooks between the recipe HIGH and LOW temperatures. Recipes indicating HI must be cooked 2-4 hours more than the longest recipe time given. A 6-8 hour recipe needs to be cooked 10-12 hours. Recipes indicating LOW must be cooked about 2 hours less than the times given. A 6-8 hour recipe needs to be cooked 4-6 hours.

Cleaning—Do not immerse pot. Fill it with warm soapy water to soak off stubborn food. Teflon II makes the pot easy to clean. Use and Care chapter tells how to clean Teflon II.

Reliable Temperatures

Reliable 5½-quart Crockery Slow Cooker

Usable capacity 5 quarts. This extra-large pot is designed for large recipes. The deep crockery liner has a painted-metal case with an attached cord. Wraparound heating elements in this pot are designed for cooking large quantities and the inside and outside of the pot become very hot. Use hot pads and *caution* in handling the pot and glass lid.

Temperature and Recipe Times—Our tests showed much higher temperatures than for other brands because this pot is designed for large quantity recipes. To use this pot with our recipe times and temperature settings, double 4-6 serving recipe quantities or reduce cooking times. Recipes indicating LOW must be reduced about an hour for a 6-hour recipe. Recipes that cook 4-8 hours on HIGH must be reduced ¼ or more of the indicated time to avoid overcooking.

Cleaning—This pot is not immersible. Fill the empty pot with warm soapy water to soak off stubborn food. Follow the Use and Care chapter recommendations for cleaning crockery. Use warm soapy water and a damp cloth to wipe off the sides.

3½ quart

Rival 3 1/2-qt. Temperatures

Rival Crock-Pots

All models have crockery liners with clear glass or Lexan plastic lids. Wraparound heating elements provide even heating from top to bottom. Cords are attached on some models, detachable with the temperature control on others. Accessories include a metal rack and baking pans with lids. The painted metal outside surface and glass lid of all models except the 3, 4½, and 5-qt. models get very hot and you should use hot pads and caution in handling the pot and lid. The Lexan surface of the 3, 4½, and 5-qt. models remains reasonably cool, even when the pot has been on all day.

Temperature & Recipe Times—Temperature settings of LOW and HIGH are exactly as found in the recipes. Cooking times are the same as provided in the recipes. Detachable temperature control units must be pushed all the way into the pot. Turn the knob *exactly* to LOW or HIGH or the pot will not heat.

Cleaning—These pots are not immersible. Fill the empty pot with warm water to soak off stubborn food. Follow the Use and Care chapter recommendations for cleaning crockery.

2-quart Stoneware Cooker—Usable capacity 1¾ quarts. This pot is good for one or two people. Ingredients for 4 to 5 serving recipes must be cut in half to fit this pot.

4½ & 5 quart

Rival Crock-Pots

3-quart Casserole Cooker/Server—Usable capacity 2½ quarts. Has removable crockery bowl (10-inch diameter) which is oven proof and dishwasher safe. When you use the bowl in the refrigerator, allow it to warm up to room temperature before re-heating. You can put the bowl in warm—not hot— water to hasten warming. Do not turn pot ON before inserting bowl or you may break the crock. Four to five serving recipes fit this pot.

3½-quart Electric Slow Cooker—Usable capacity 3 quarts. Use 4 to 5 serving recipes with this popular model.

3½-quart Deluxe Buffet Cooker—Usable capacity 3 quarts. Use 4 to 5 serving recipes with this pot. The feet and handles and a detachable cord are features which are different from the standard model.

4½- and 5-quart Deluxe Cooker/Server—Usable capacity 4 quarts. Both models are exactly the same. The 10-inch-diameter pot will hold most roasts, chickens and large meals. Some 4 to 5 serving recipes can be doubled for use in this pot. Cooking times stay the same.

4-quart integrated model

Sears 4-quart Crockery Cooker (also Simpsons)

Usable capacity 3½ quarts. This crockery pot has a glass lid, painted metal outside finish and attached cord.

The sides and lid get very hot so use a pot holder to remove the lid. Pick up the pot only by the handles.

Temperature & Recipe Times—Heating from the sides provides even heat distribution from top to bottom. This pot fits recipe temperatures and cooking times exactly. The temperature switch has two positions, MED and HI. For recipes in this book MED equals LOW and HI equals HIGH.

Cleaning—Do not immerse to clean. Fill empty pot with water to soak off stubborn food. Use and Care chapter tells how to clean crockery.

Sears Tray Model Crockery Cookers (also Simpsons)

These cookers have an electric heating base and a separate crockery pot with glass lid. The painted rectangular heating base has wooden handles and an attached cord. The pot sits in a shallow well in the heating base.

The crockery pots are dishwasher and oven safe, but you should not place the pot on any stove burner because that could break the pot. Always put ingredients into the pot *before* placing it on the heating base. Turn on the heat only after the crockery pot with contents has been placed in the heating well.

WARNING: At least one cup of liquid must be part of any recipe used in these pots. Do not let the pot operate dry for baking and do not let all of the liquid evaporate or the pot will overheat and probably break.

5-quart tray model

Sears 4-quart Crockery Cooker (also Simpsons)

The heating base may be used to warm food in pots or pans, but don't use the heating surface for a griddle. Both the pot and base get very hot, so use hot pads or mitts to handle either one. Do not attempt to move the base without pot holders, even though there are wooden handles. These wooden ends offer little protection against burning your hands. The heating bases smoke at first as the heating element warms up and burns off protective coatings.

Temperature & Recipe Times—For recipes in this book, set the 5-quart temperature controls to 2 for LOW and 3 for HIGH. Position 1 is too cool to cook food because it is designed for warming. Use the times given in the recipes. See special temperature note with 2½-quart pot described below.

Cleaning—Never immerse the heating base in water. Wipe it clean with a damp cloth when it is completely cool. The Use and Care chapter tells how to clean crockery.

2½-quart—Usable capacity 2 quarts. This pot is ideal for one or two people. To use the 4 to 6 serving recipes in this book, reduce the ingredients by ½. Setting 3 on the control is equal to LOW in the recipes. Because this pot will not attain high temperatures equal to the HIGH settings recommended in some recipes, use only those recipes which cook on LOW for the entire period.

5-quart—Usable capacity 4½ quarts.

Sunbeam Crocker Cooker Temperatures

325°–350° F. SETTING

LEFT OF RED CROCKERY BAND

Sunbeam Crocker Cooker Fryer

Usable capacity 4 quarts. This unit cooks slowly and has a removable crockery pot. The heavy-wall pot provides even heat distribution, even though heating is only from the bottom. A large lip on the pot makes it easy to handle. It is dishwasher safe and oven proof. This unit is both a cooker and a fryer with a Teflon-coated cooking surface. It can be used for deep frying.

Temperature & Recipe Times—For recipes in this book use 200°F. for LOW. There is no 200°F. marker on the dial, so set it just left of the red CROCKERY band. For HIGH, set it between 325°F. and 350°F. Cooking times in the recipes are exactly right for this pot.

Cleaning—To clean, remove the empty pot and fill with warm water to soak off stubborn food. The slow cooker/fryer heating portion does not get very dirty with slow cooking. Wiping with a damp cloth will usually clean off any spilled food. Do not immerse the cooker/fryer unit.

Sunbeam Crocker Frypan Temperatures

300° F. SETTING

200° F. SETTING

Sunbeam Crocker Frypan

Usable capacity 2 quarts. This Teflon-coated electric frypan has a removable crockery insert. The fryer and insert are square-shaped and the lid is domed so the pot can hold pieces of meat or poultry somewhat taller than the depth of the pot. This model does not cook like other crockery-lined slow-cooking pots because the shallow crock liner exposes a lot of the food surface. Heating this shallow crock from the bottom heats the food unevenly and tends to cause the food to dry out. This causes faster cooking and requires frequent stirring to prevent sticking. Meats must be turned to ensure even doneness. Some recipes, especially soups and beans, can be used successfully in this pot.

Temperature & Recipe Times—For recipes in this book, use 200°F. for LOW and 300°F. for HIGH. Cooking times in the recipes may be shortened $\frac{1}{4}$ to $\frac{1}{2}$ for use with this pot.

Cleaning—Remove the empty crock and fill with warm water to soak off stubborn food. The frypan heating portion does not get very dirty with slow cooking. Wiping with a damp cloth will usually clean off any spilled food. Do not immerse the frypan unit. The Use and Care chapter details cleaning hints for crockery and Teflon.

K-mart LaCuisine Sim•R•Pot

Van Wyck Sim·R·Pot
Robeson Sim·R·Pot
K-Mart LaCuisine Sim·R·Pot

Usable capacity 3 quarts. This popular pot fits most 4-5 serving recipes well. The pot has a painted metal outside surface with a white-glass liner and a clear-glass lid. The cord is attached. Do not touch the outside metal surface because it gets very hot. Plastic handles remain cool enough to handle, but it is best to use hot pads whenever you move or lift the pot or lid. Heating elements are wrapped around the pot.

Temperature & Recipe Times—Make sure to turn the control switch exactly to Sim·R·LO or Sim·R·HI. For recipes that cook on LOW, use times given in our recipes. Recipes which cook on HIGH will require at least an additional 2 hours and perhaps more.

Cleaning—Because this pot is not immersible, fill it with warm soapy water to soak off stubborn food. Wipe off the outside with a damp cloth. The Use and Care chapter explains how to clean glass liners.

Wards & Van Wyck 4-qt. Temperatures

Van Wyck Sim·R·Ware (also Wards and others)

Usable capacity 4 quarts. These glass-lined pots have glass lids. Wraparound heating element provides even heating from top to bottom. The cord is detachable. The outside of the pot and lid get very hot. Use a pot holder or mitts to remove the lid and pick up the pot only with the handles. This pot was supplied in 11 different trims for different stores and chain stores. It was discontinued in 1975.

Temperature & Recipe Times—As you can see in the temperature chart, this pot does not get very hot. Use the HIGH setting whenever the recipe calls for LOW. Recipes requiring HIGH settings will have to be cooked several extra hours to be done.

Cleaning—Do not immerse this unit in water. Fill empty cooker with warm soapy water to wash it. See Use and Care chapter for hints on cleaning the glass liner without using abrasives.

Wards 5 1/2-qt. Temperatures

Wards 5½-quart Crockery Slow Cooker

Usable capacity 5 quarts. This extra-large pot is designed for large recipes. The deep crockery liner has a painted metal case with an attached cord. Wraparound heating elements in this pot are designed for cooking large quantities and the inside and outside of the pot becomes very hot. Use hot pads and *caution* in handling the pot and glass lid.

Temperature and Recipe Times—Our tests showed much higher temperatures than for other brands because this pot is designed for large quantity recipes. To use this pot with our recipe times and temperature settings, double 4-6 serving recipe quantities or reduce cooking times. Recipes indicating LOW must be reduced about an hour for a 6-hour recipe. Recipes that cook 4-8 hours on HIGH must be reduced ¼ or more of the indicated time to avoid overcooking.

Cleaning—This pot is not immersible. Fill the empty pot with warm soapy water to soak off stubborn food. Follow the Use and Care chapter recommendations for cleaning crockery. Use warm soapy water and a damp cloth to wipe off the sides.

Wear·Ever Pokey·Pot

Usable capacity 3 quarts. This pot is available with either a removable brown ceramic crock or a white-glass liner. The units cook exactly alike. The removable container sets in a separate heating pot containing fully insulated heating elements. The heating pot is aluminum with a porcelain finish. The temperature control detaches with its cord. The lid is glass. The liners are dishwasher and oven-safe, but you should not place them on a stove burner or electric element because this will break the crockery or glass. Do not turn the heating pot on before inserting the crock or glass liner.

Temperature & Recipe Times—This pot fits our recipe temperatures and times for LOW. Shorten recipe times on HIGH by 2 hours or more.

Cleaning—Do not immerse the heating pot in water. Wipe it clean with a damp cloth when it is completely cool. The Use and Care chapter tells how to clean crockery and glass liners.

West Bend Colonial Crock Slo-Cooker (in foreground)
and Bean Pot

Usable capacity 2 quarts. This stoneware pot and lid are used with a separate heating base. Do not heat the base before setting the pot on it or you may break the crock. The pot can be used in your oven at temperatures up to 425°F. *if you pre-heat the oven to 425°F. first.* Do not use the pot directly on gas or electric ranges or it will break. The heating base may be used as a warming and cooking unit for other pans or coffee makers, but do not use the heating surface as a griddle. Do not try to carry or move the heating base when it is hot. Carry the pot and handle the lid with hot pads.

Temperature & Recipe Times—The Colonial Crock Slo-Cooker temperature control has settings L, 1, 2, 3, 4 and H, but no OFF position. Unplug the cord to turn OFF. Set the temperature indicator to H and use those recipes which cook only on LOW because this pot will not attain temperatures equal to the HIGH setting on other pots. Bean pot does not have variable control. Use recipes which cook on LOW.

Cleaning—Follow Use and Care chapter directions for crockery. Do not soak the pot or lid for long periods of time because the non-glazed pot bottom and inside of lid will absorb water. Before storing, let pot and lid stand *inverted* until completely dry. When washed in a dishwasher the normal drying cycle will dry out the stoneware.

West Bend 3 1/2 qt. Temperatures

West Bend Home Maid Slo-Cooker

Usable capacity 3½ quarts. This porcelain coated steel pot has a Teflon II coated cooking surface. The lid is glass. The pot can be used in the oven at temperatures up to 350°F, *if you preheat the oven to 350°F first.* You can also use the pot on gas or electric ranges, provided flames or heat do not come up the sides to damage the handles.

The heating base may be used as a warming and cooking unit for other pans or coffee makers, but do not use the heating surface as a griddle. Do not try to carry or move the base while it is hot. Carry the pot or handle the lid only with hot pads.

Temperature & Recipe Times—The temperature control has settings from 1 to 5, but no OFF position. Unplug the cord to turn OFF. Use the 3 setting and the same times for recipes which cook on Low. Recipes calling for a HIGH setting should be cooked on the 4 setting for about 3-4 more hours.

Cleaning—Folow Use and Care chapter directions for Teflon II. The pot is immersible and can be cleaned in the sink or dishwasher. If you use a dishwasher, recondition the cooking surface with cooking oil before re-using the pot. Do not immerse heating base in water. Wipe it clean with a damp cloth when it is cool.

West Bend Lazy Day Slo-Cooker

Usable capacity 5 quarts. This porcelain-coated steel pot and lid are used with a separate heating base. The pot can be used in the oven at temperatures up to 350°F. Preheat the oven before placing the pot in it because preheating temperatures may exceed 350°F., which could damage the plastic handles. You can also use the pot on gas or electric ranges, provided flames or heat do not come up the side of the pot to damage the handles.

The heating base may be used as a warming and cooking unit for other pans or coffee makers, but do not use the heating surface as a griddle. Do not try to carry or move the heating base when it is hot. Carry the pot only by the handles.

Temperature & Recipe Times——The temperature control has settings from 1 to 5, but no OFF position. Unplug the cord to turn off. For recipes in this book, set dial at 2 for LOW and 4 for HIGH. Recipe times are the same as those in the recipes.

Cleaning——Follow Use and Care chapter directions for porcelain. The pot can be cleaned in the sink or dishwasher as it is immersible. Do not immerse heating base in water. Wipe it clean with a damp cloth when it is cool.

BEEF

Slow-cooked beef is fabulous! You can stretch your penny-pincher budget by buying cheaper, less tender cuts. The pot makes them super tender—and you end up with more flavor and vitamins. Surprise! You get less shrinkage than with other cooking methods.

Here are some secrets for slow cooking beef successfully. The first: Some vegetables take as long or longer to cook than beef. If you plan a beef dish with large chunks of carrots or celery, place these in the bottom or around the sides of the pot. And, cover them with liquid such as water, bouillon or tomato sauce. You may want to cut them slightly smaller than usual. Slow cookers are notoriously slow when cooking vegetables and smaller pieces cook faster.

Another secret: The good juices of the meat don't evaporate. As a result, you get more liquid with that rich, meaty flavor—a special treat for sauce and gravy lovers. In most cases you can stir in cornstarch or dissolve flour after the meat is done. Then cook on HIGH for a few minutes to thicken the gravy.

It is not necessary to brown meat before you cook. But, if the meat is fatty, browning first and pouring off the excess fat is usually helpful. Ordinarily, you can place most beef cuts directly in the bottom of the pot with the seasonings and vegetables. But, if the meat is really fatty or you don't want it to cook in the juices, put it on a rack in the bottom of the pot.

You will notice a wide range of cooking times for all of the beef recipes. That's another advantage of slow cookers — you can take off in the morning, leave the meat cooking most of the day and not worry about it sticking, burning or overcooking should you return later than expected. The low temperature is so low than an hour or two makes very little difference in slow-cooking recipes.

How do you decide when the beef is done? Cook until the minimum time suggested for the recipe. Then, just remove the meat from the slow-cooking pot and stick it with a fork to see if it is as tender as your family prefers. The thickness of the cut of beef, distribution of fat and amount of bone will change the cooking time, so always check before assuming the meat is ready to serve.

CREOLE STEAK STRIPS

1½ lbs. boneless round
  steak
Salt and pepper
1 onion, chopped
1 cup sliced celery
1 cup seasoned tomato
  juice
2 tsp. Worcestershire
  sauce
⅛ tsp. garlic powder
1 medium green pepper,
  chopped
1 (10-oz.) package frozen
  or 1½ cups fresh okra
1 (2½-oz.) can sliced
  mushrooms, drained
Carrot curls (optional)

Cut steak into strips about ½ inch wide and 2 inches long. Sprinkle with salt and pepper. Place in slow-cooking pot with onion, celery, tomato juice, Worcestershire sauce, and garlic powder. Cover and cook on low 6 to 8 hours. Turn control to high. Add green peppers and partially thawed okra and mushrooms. Cover and cook on high for 30 minutes or until okra is done. Garnish with carrot curls if desired. Serve over rice. Makes 5 to 6 servings.

MEXICAN BEEF

1½ to 2 lbs. boneless
  round steak
1 clove garlic, minced
¼ tsp. pepper
½ tsp. salt
1 tbs. chili powder
1 tbs. prepared mustard
1 onion, chopped
1 beef bouillon cube,
  crushed
1 (16-oz.) can tomatoes,
  cut up
1 (16-oz.) can kidney
  beans, drained

Spread meat with mixture of garlic, pepper, salt, chili powder, and mustard. Cut into ½-inch wide strips. Place in slow-cooking pot. Cover with onion, bouillon cube, and tomatoes. Cover and cook on low for 6 to 8 hours. Turn control to high. Add beans and cook, covered, for 30 minutes. Serve on bed of rice. Makes 5 to 6 servings.

Creole Steak Strips
Courtesy National Livestock & Meat Board

ROUND STEAK WITH RICH GRAVY

2 to 2½ lbs. round steak
1 (1½-oz.) package onion
  soup mix
¼ cup water

1 (10½-oz.) can
  condensed cream of
  mushroom soup

Cut steak into 5 or 6 serving-size pieces. Place in slow-cooking pot. Add dry onion soup mix, water, and condensed mushroom soup. Cover and cook on low for 6 to 8 hours. Excellent when served with mashed potatoes. Makes 5 or 6 servings.

ROUND STEAK ITALIANO

1½ lbs. round steak
1 tsp. salt
½ tsp. oregano
¼ tsp. pepper

1 (15½-oz.) jar spaghetti
  sauce with mushrooms
1 (16-oz.) can whole small
  onions, drained

Cut steak into 5 or 6 serving-size pieces. Coat with salt, oregano, and pepper. In slow-cooking pot, pour spaghetti sauce over meat. Cover and cook on low for 7 to 9 hours or until meat is tender. Turn control to high; add onions. Cook on high for 10 to 15 minutes. Serve with Italian green beans and toasted garlic cheese bread. Makes 5 to 6 servings.

BUDGET BEEF STROGANOFF

1½ to 2 lbs. round steak	1½ cups beef bouillon
1 tsp. salt	1 tbs. catsup
⅛ tsp. pepper	2 tbs. dry white wine
1 onion, sliced	¼ lb. fresh mushrooms,
¼ tsp. garlic salt	sliced
1 tbs. Worcestershire	⅓ cup flour
sauce	1 cup dairy sour cream

Cut steak into ¼-inch strips. Coat with salt and pepper. Drop into bottom of slow-cooking pot with onion. Mix garlic salt, Worcestershire sauce, bouillon, and catsup. Pour over meat. Cover and cook on low for 6 to 8 hours or until tender. Turn control to high. Add wine and mushrooms. Dissolve flour in small amount of water. Add to meat mixture, stirring until blended. Cook on high for 15 minutes or until slightly thickened. Stir in sour cream; turn off heat. Serve with rice or noodles. Makes 5 to 6 servings.

SWEDISH STYLE STEAK

2 to 2½ lbs. boneless	1 bouillon cube, crumbled
round steak	½ cup water
Salt and pepper	¼ cup flour
1 tsp. dill weed	¼ cup water
1 medium onion, sliced	1 cup dairy sour cream

Cut steak into serving-size pieces. Sprinkle with salt and pepper. Place in slow-cooking pot. Add dill, onion, bouillon cube and ½ cup water. Cover and cook on low for 6 to 8 hours. Remove meat. Thicken juices with flour dissolved in ¼ cup cold water. Turn control to high; cook 10 minutes or until slightly thickened. Stir in sour cream. Turn off heat. Serve sauce over meat, with mashed potatoes or noodles. Makes 6 to 8 servings.

SWISS BEEF BIRDS

2 lbs. round steak,
  ½-inch thick
2 medium carrots
1 large dill pickle
2 tbs. flour
1 tsp. salt

¼ tsp. pepper
⅛ tsp. garlic salt
2 tbs. salad oil
1 (8-oz.) can tomato sauce
1 small onion, chopped
2 tbs. minced parsley

With meat mallet, pound steak until ¼ inch thick; cut into 5 or 6 serving pieces. Cut each carrot into thin sticks and the pickle into 5 or 6 strips. Place several carrot sticks and one pickle stick on each piece of meat. Beginning at narrow end, roll up, securing with small skewers or toothpicks. Mix flour with salt, pepper, and garlic salt; coat rolls, reserving remaining mixture. In large skillet or slow-cooking pot with browning unit, brown meat rolls in hot oil. Pour off excess fat. Place browned meat in slow-cooking pot. Mix tomato sauce with reserved flour; stir in onion. Pour over meat. Cover and simmer on low for 7 to 9 hours or until tender. Sprinkle with parsley. Makes 5 or 6 servings.

SWISS STEAK

1½ to 2 lbs. round steak
2 tbs. flour
1 tsp. salt
⅛ tsp. pepper
2 tbs. salad oil
1 (16-oz.) can tomatoes,
  cut up

1 large onion, sliced
1 stalk celery, thinly
  sliced
1 tbs. thick bottled steak
  sauce

Cut steak into serving-size pieces. Coat with flour, salt, and pepper. In large skillet or slow-cooking pot with browning unit, brown meat in oil. Pour off excess fat. In slow-cooking pot, combine meat with tomatoes, onion, celery, and steak sauce. Cover pot and cook on low for 6 to 8 hours or until tender. Thicken juices with additional flour dissolved in a small amount of water, if desired. Makes 5 to 6 servings.

CHINESE PEPPER STEAK

1 to 1½ lbs. round steak
2 tbs. oil
1 clove garlic, minced
½ tsp. salt
¼ tsp. pepper
¼ cup soy sauce
1 tsp. sugar
1 cup fresh or canned
  bean sprouts, drained

1 cup canned tomatoes,
  cut up
2 green peppers, seeded
  and cut into strips
1 tbs. cornstarch
2 tbs. cold water
4 green onions, sliced

Slice steak into narrow strips. In skillet or slow-cooking pot with browning unit, brown steak in oil. Combine with garlic, salt, pepper, soy sauce, and sugar in slow-cooking pot. Cook on low 6 to 8 hours. Turn control to high. Add bean sprouts, tomatoes, and green peppers. Dissolve cornstarch in water. Stir into pot. Cover and cook on high 15-20 minutes or until thickened. Sprinkle with onions. Makes 4 to 5 servings.

FLEMISH CARBONADES

2 to 3 lbs. boneless chuck,
  cut into 1-inch cubes
½ cup flour
¼ cup butter or
  margarine
1 onion, sliced

1 tsp. salt
⅛ tsp. pepper
1 clove garlic, minced
2 cups beer
¼ cup flour

Coat beef with ½ cup flour. In large skillet or slow-cooking pot with browning unit, brown meat in melted butter. Drain off excess fat. In slow-cooking pot, combine meat with onion, salt, pepper, garlic, and beer. Cover and cook on low for 5 to 7 hours or until meat is tender. Turn control to high. Dissolve remaining ¼ cup flour in small amount of water. Stir into meat mixture; cook on high for 20 to 30 minutes. Makes 5 to 7 servings.

NEW ENGLAND CHUCK ROAST

1 (3-lb.) beef chuck roast
1 tsp. monosodium
glutamate
1 tsp. salt
¼ tsp. pepper
2 onions, cut into quarters
4 carrots, cut into quarters

1 stalk celery, cut into
eight chunks
1 bay leaf
2 tbs. vinegar
5 cups water
1 small cabbage cut into
wedges

Sauce:

3 tbs. butter or margarine
1 tbs. instant minced
onion
2 tbs. flour
1½ cups reserved beef
broth

2 tbs. prepared
horseradish
½ tsp. salt

Sprinkle meat with seasonings. Place onions, carrots, and celery in slow-cooking pot. Top with meat. Add bay leaf, vinegar and water. Cover pot and cook on low for 5 to 7 hours or until meat is tender. Remove meat; turn to high. Add cabbage wedges; cover and cook on high for 15 to 20 minutes or until cabbage is done. Meanwhile melt butter in saucepan. Stir in instant onion and flour. Drain 1½ cups broth out of slow-cooking pot. Pour broth, horseradish and salt into saucepan. Cook over low heat, stirring constantly, until thickened and smooth. Serve sauce with roast and vegetables. Makes 6 servings.

CHINESE BEEF AND PEA PODS

1 (1 to 1½ lbs.) flank steak
1 (10½-oz.) can
  condensed beef
  consommé
¼ cup soy sauce
¼ tsp. ground ginger
1 bunch green onions,
  sliced
2 tbs. cornstarch
2 tbs. cold water
1 (7-oz.) package frozen
  Chinese pea pods,
  partially thawed

Thinly slice flank steak diagonally across the grain. Combine strips in slow-cooking pot with consommé, soy sauce, ginger and onions. Cover and cook on low for 5 to 7 hours. Turn control to high. Stir in cornstarch that has been dissolved in the cold water. Cook on high for 10 to 15 minutes or until thickened. Drop in pea pods the last 5 minutes. Serve over hot rice. Makes 4 to 5 servings.

TERIYAKI STEAK

2 to 2½ lbs. boneless
  chuck steak
1 tsp. ground ginger
1 tbs. sugar
2 tbs. oil
½ cup soy sauce
1 clove garlic, crushed

Cut steak into ⅛-inch thick slices. Combine remaining ingredients in small bowl. Place meat in slow-cooking pot. Pour sauce over. Cover and cook on low for 6 to 8 hours. Serve with rice. Makes 5 to 6 servings.

FLANK STEAK IN MUSHROOM SAUCE

1 (1 to 1½ lb.) flank steak
¼ cup sauterne wine
1 tbs. soy sauce
1 clove garlic, minced
1 (10½-oz.) can beef
  broth
1 tbs. catsup

1 tsp. prepared mustard
1 tbs. instant minced
  onion
2 tbs. cornstarch
2 tbs. water
¼ lb. fresh mushrooms,
  sliced

Place steak in slow-cooking pot. Combine sauterne, soy sauce, garlic, broth, catsup, mustard, and onion; pour over steak. Cover and cook on low for 6 to 8 hours. Dissolve cornstarch in water; stir into pot. Add mushrooms. Turn control to high; cover and cook on high 20 to 30 minutes or until mushrooms are done. Makes 4 to 5 servings.

FLANK STEAK CREOLE

1½ to 2 lbs. flank steak
Salt and pepper
2 tbs. chopped green
  pepper
2 tbs. chopped onion
1 tbs. tomato paste
½ tsp. prepared
  horseradish

¼ tsp. sugar
½ cup water
2 cups herb-seasoned
  stuffing mix
2 tbs. cornstarch
¼ cup cold water
1 tbs. tomato paste

Score one side of meat. Sprinkle with salt and pepper. Combine green pepper, onion, 1 tbs. tomato paste, horseradish, sugar, ½ cup water, and stuffing. Spoon stuffing mixture down middle of unscored side of flank steak. Fold ends over and overlap long sides; skewer together. Place on metal rack or trivet in slow-cooking pot. Cover and cook on low for 8 to 10 hours. Remove meat. Turn control to high. Dissolve cornstarch in ¼ cup cold water; stir in 1 tbs. tomato paste. Add to juices in pot. Cook on high for 15 to 20 minutes or until slightly thickened. Slice steak across the grain. Pass sauce with the steak. Makes 4 to 5 servings.

STUFFED FLANK STEAK

1½ cups packaged bread stuffing

1 (3-oz.) can sliced mushrooms with juice

2 tbs. melted butter or margarine

2 tbs. grated Parmesan cheese

1 (1 to 1½-lb.) flank steak, scored on both sides

2 tbs. salad oil

Sauce:

1 (¾-oz.) package brown gravy mix

¼ cup dry red wine

2 tbs. minced green onions

¼ cup currant jelly

Combine bread stuffing with mushrooms and juice, butter, and cheese. Spread over flank steak; roll up like jelly roll. Fasten with skewers or string. Pour oil in slow-cooking pot. Roll steak in oil, coating all sides. *For Sauce:* Prepare gravy mix according to package directions. Pour gravy, wine, and onions over meat. Cover and cook on low 8 to 10 hours. Remove meat from pot; slice. Add jelly to sauce and stir until dissolved. Serve over meat. Makes 4 to 5 servings.

1/Score flank to make it flexible to roll.

2/Spread stuffing over flank steak. Roll up like jelly roll and fasten with skewers or string.

3/Pour sauce over meat.

FRUITED FLANK STEAK

1 (1 to 1½-lb.) flank steak
Salt and pepper
1 (30-oz.) can fruit
  cocktail
1 tbs. salad oil

1 tbs. lemon juice
¼ cup bottled teriyaki
  sauce
1 tsp. vinegar
1 clove garlic, minced

Sprinkle flank steak with salt and pepper; place in slow-cooking pot. Drain fruit cocktail, saving ¼ cup syrup. Combine ¼ cup syrup with remaining ingredients; pour over steak in pot. Cover and cook on low for 7 to 9 hours or until tender. Add drained fruit the last few minutes. Lift out of pot; place on platter. With sharp knife, cut thin slices of meat across the grain. Serve hot. Makes 4 to 5 servings.

BEEF BURGUNDY

2 slices bacon, chopped
2 lbs. sirloin tip or round
  steak, cut into 1-inch
  cubes
¼ cup flour
1 tsp. salt
½ tsp. seasoned salt
¼ tsp. marjoram
¼ tsp. thyme

¼ tsp. pepper
1 clove garlic, minced
1 beef bouillon cube,
  crushed
1 cup Burgundy wine
¼ lb. fresh mushrooms,
  sliced
2 tbs. cornstarch
  (optional)

In large skillet or slow-cooking pot with browning unit, cook bacon several minutes. Remove bacon and set aside. Coat beef with flour and brown on all sides in bacon mixture. Combine steak, bacon drippings, cooked bacon, seasonings, bouillon, and Burgundy in slow-cooking pot. Cover and cook on low for 6 to 8 hours or until meat is tender. Turn control to high. Add mushrooms; cook on high 15 minutes. To thicken sauce, if desired, add cornstarch (dissolved in 2 tbs. cold water) with mushrooms. Makes 6 servings.

RANCH STYLE BEEF

2 lbs. boneless beef stew
   meat, cut into 1½-inch
   cubes
12 to 14 small white
   onions
4 whole cloves
2 tbs. brown sugar
1½ tsp. salt
½ tsp. bottled brown
   gravy sauce
1 tbs. red wine vinegar
1 bay leaf
⅛ tsp. thyme
¾ cup water
¼ cup flour

In slow-cooking pot, alternate beef and onions; stick
cloves into 4 onions. Sprinkle with sugar and salt.
Combine gravy sauce, vinegar, bay leaf, thyme, and
water. Pour over meat. Cover and cook on low for 5
to 7 hours or until tender. Turn control to high. Dissolve flour in small amount of water. Stir into meat
juices. Cook on high for 15 to 20 minutes. Makes 6
servings.

FARM STYLE STEW

1½ lbs. beef stew meat,
   cut into 1-inch cubes
1 tsp. salt
¼ tsp. pepper
½ tsp. paprika
½ tsp. seasoned salt
4 medium zucchini, cut
   into 1-inch slices
2 cups hot water
2 tbs. bottled steak sauce
1 (17-oz.) can whole
   kernel corn, drained
3 tbs. cornstarch
3 tbs. cold water

Sprinkle beef with salt, pepper, paprika, and seasoned
salt. Place in slow-cooking pot with zucchini; pour hot
water and steak sauce over. Cover and cook on low for
7 to 9 hours or until tender. Turn control to high. Stir
in corn. Dissolve cornstarch in cold water; add to meat
mixture. Cook on high for 15 to 20 minutes. Makes 5
to 6 servings.

OLD-FASHIONED BEEF STEW

2 lbs. beef stew meat, cut
  into 1½-inch cubes
½ cup flour
2 tbs. oil
1 bay leaf
1 tbs. Worcestershire
  sauce
1 onion, chopped
1 cup beef bouillon
¼ tsp. pepper
2 tsp. salt
1 tsp. sugar

6 carrots, peeled and
  sliced or quartered
1 cup sliced celery
4 potatoes, peeled and
  cut into eighths
12 small white onions
2 medium turnips, peeled
  and quartered (optional)
4 cups water
1 cup cooked okra
  (optional)

Coat meat with flour; set excess flour aside. In large
skillet or slow-cooking pot with browning unit, heat
oil. Brown meat on all sides. In slow-cooking pot, combine browned beef, bay leaf, Worcestershire sauce,
chopped onion, bouillon, pepper, salt, sugar, and vegetables. Pour water over all. Cover and cook on low 8
to 10 hours. Turn control on high. Thicken with flour
left over from coating (about ¼ cup) dissolved in a
small amount of water. Add okra if desired. Cover and
cook on high 10 to 15 minutes or until slightly thickened. Makes 6 to 8 servings.

OXTAIL STEW

4 lbs. oxtails, cut into
  2-inch lengths
¼ cup flour
Salt and pepper
2 tbs. salad oil
1 medium tomato, peeled
  and chopped
1 onion, chopped

3 carrots, chopped
2 turnips, chopped
1 clove garlic, crushed
1 bay leaf
3 cups beef bouillon
1 cup port wine
½ tsp. pepper
2 leeks, sliced

Coat meat with flour; sprinkle with salt and pepper. In
large skillet or slow-cooking pot with browning unit,
brown meat in oil. Drain off excess fat. Combine
browned meat in slow-cooking pot with remaining ingredients. Cover and cook on low for 7 to 9 hours. Remove bay leaf and oxtails. Cut meat off bones; dice
and return to stew. Let stand a few minutes; skim excess fat off top.* Makes 6 to 8 servings.

*If time permits, refrigerate stew; skim off excess cold
fat and then reheat stew at serving time.

BARBECUED BEEF & BEANS

2 to 2½ lbs. beef stew
  meat, cut into 1-inch
  cubes
Salt and pepper
1 cup smoke-flavored
  barbecue sauce

1 cup beef bouillon
2 (1-lb.) cans dry lima
  beans, drained

Sprinkle beef with salt and pepper. Place in slow-
cooking pot with barbecue sauce and bouillon. Cover
and cook on low for 4 to 6 hours. Add drained beans
and cook on high 15 to 20 minutes. Makes 6 servings.

SOUTHWESTERN BEEF & BEANS

1 lb. dried pinto beans	1 medium onion, chopped
6 cups cold water	2 cloves garlic, minced
½ lb. salt pork, cut up	1 (6-oz.) can tomato paste
1 lb. lean chuck steak, cut into 1-inch cubes	1½ tbs. chili powder
1 red chili pepper or ½ tsp. crushed red pepper	1 tsp. salt
	1 tsp. cumin seed
	½ tsp. marjoram leaves

Soak beans in water overnight. Brown salt pork in skillet or slow-cooking pot with browning unit. In slow-cooking pot, combine soaked beans (with water), browned pork, and remaining ingredients. Cover and cook on low for 9 to 10 hours. Makes 8 servings.

SPANISH STYLE LIVER

2 lbs. sliced beef or calves liver	1 (1-lb.) can stewed tomatoes
4 slices bacon, cut in half	1 tsp. salt
½ cup chopped carrot	⅛ tsp. pepper
½ cup chopped celery	1 small bay leaf
1 small onion, sliced	

Place liver in slow-cooking pot. Arrange bacon on top. Mix remaining ingredients and pour over liver. Cover and cook on low 6 to 8 hours. Remove bay leaf. Makes 5 to 6 servings.

MARCO POLO SHORT RIBS

4 lbs. beef short ribs
1 large tomato, chopped
1 cup beef bouillon
¼ cup Burgundy wine
1 tbs. instant minced
   onion
2 tbs. prepared
   horseradish
1 tsp. salt
¼ tsp. pepper
¼ tsp. ground ginger
2 tbs. cornstarch

In large skillet or slow-cooking pot with browning unit, brown short ribs; drain off fat. In slow-cooking pot, combine meat with remaining ingredients except cornstarch. Cover and cook on low for 6 to 8 hours. Turn control to high. Remove meat from pot. Skim excess fat off top of meat broth. Dissolve cornstarch in small amount of cold water; stir into meat juices in pot. Cook on high for 15 to 20 minutes or until slightly thickened. Serve over meat. Makes 4 to 6 servings.

HOME-STYLE SHORT RIBS

3 to 4 lbs. lean beef short
   ribs
4 potatoes, peeled and
   quartered
4 carrots, peeled and
   quartered
1 onion, sliced
2 tbs. vinegar
2 tsp. sugar
1 tbs. horseradish
1 tbs. prepared mustard
2 tbs. catsup
1 cup beef bouillon
1 tsp. salt
¼ tsp. pepper
¼ cup flour

In large skillet or slow-cooking pot with browning unit, brown short ribs; drain off excess fat. Place potatoes, carrots and onion in slow-cooking pot. Arrange browned ribs over vegetables. Combine vinegar, sugar, horseradish, mustard, catsup, bouillon, salt and pepper. Pour over meat. Cover and cook on low for 6 to 8 hours or until meat is tender. Remove short ribs and vegetables. Turn control to high. Dissolve flour in small amount of water. Stir into sauce; cook on high for 10 to 15 minutes or until thickened. Serve with meat and vegetables. Makes 4 to 6 servings.

MEXICAN STYLE SHORT RIBS

3 to 4 lbs. beef short ribs
1 (10½-oz.) can beef
  consommé
1 (1¼-oz.) package taco
  seasoning mix

¼ cup chopped green
  pepper

In large skillet or slow-cooking pot with browning unit, brown short ribs; pour off excess fat. Mix beef consommé with dry taco mix; add green pepper. In slow-cooking pot, pour sauce over ribs. Cover and cook on low for 6 to 8 hours. Makes 5 to 6 servings.

GERMAN SHORT RIBS

3 to 3½ lbs. beef short
  ribs
2 tbs. flour
1 tsp. salt
⅛ tsp. pepper
2 tbs. shortening
2 medium onions, sliced
½ cup dry red wine

½ cup chili sauce*
3 tbs. brown sugar
3 tbs. vinegar
1 tbs. Worcestershire
  sauce
½ tsp. dry mustard
½ tsp. chili powder
2 tbs. flour

Coat short ribs in mixture of 2 tablespoons flour with salt and pepper. Melt shortening in large skillet or slow-cooking pot with browning unit; add ribs and brown on all sides. Pour off excess fat. In slow-cooking pot, combine ribs, onions, wine, chili sauce, brown sugar, vinegar, Worcestershire sauce, mustard, and chili powder. Cover and cook on low for 6 to 8 hours. Turn control to high. Thicken with 2 tbs. flour that has been dissolved in a small amount of water. Cook on high about 10 minutes or until slightly thickened. Serve over wide noodles. Makes 5 to 6 servings.

*Bottled tomato sauce similar to catsup.

HUNGARIAN GOULASH

2 lbs. beef stew meat,
  cut into 1-inch cubes
1 large onion, sliced
1 clove garlic, minced
½ cup catsup
2 tbs. Worcestershire
  sauce

1 tbs. brown sugar
2 tsp. salt
2 tsp. paprika
½ tsp. dry mustard
1 cup water
¼ cup flour

Place meat in slow-cooking pot; cover with sliced
onion. Combine garlic, catsup, Worcestershire sauce,
sugar, salt, paprika, and mustard. Stir in water. Pour
over meat. Cover and cook on low for 9 to 10 hours.
Turn control to high. Dissolve flour in small amount
of cold water; stir into meat mixture. Cook on high 10
to 15 minutes or until slightly thickened. Serve goulash
over noodles or rice. Makes 5 to 6 servings.

OLD WORLD SAUERBRATEN

3½ to 4 lbs. beef rump
  or sirloin tip
1 cup water
1 cup vinegar
1 large onion, sliced
1 lemon, sliced
  (unpeeled)

10 whole cloves
4 bay leaves
6 whole peppercorns
2 tbs. salt
2 tbs. sugar
12 gingersnaps,
  crumbled

Place meat in deep ceramic or glass bowl. Combine
water, vinegar, onion, lemon, cloves, bay leaves,
pepper, salt, and sugar. Pour over meat. Cover and
refrigerate for 24 to 36 hours; turn meat several times
during marinating. Place beef in slow-cooking pot;
pour 1 cup marinade over meat. Cover and cook on
low 6 to 8 hours. Place meat on serving platter. Strain
meat juices and return to pot. Turn control to high.
Stir in gingersnaps; cover and cook on high for 10 to
15 minutes. Pour over meat. Makes 8 servings.

ALPHABET POT ROAST

3 to 4-lb. beef pot roast
Salt and pepper
1 (10¾-oz.) can alphabet
vegetable soup,
undiluted

½ cup dry red wine
⅛ tsp. dried basil
2 tbs. finely chopped
parsley

Sprinkle beef with salt and pepper. Place in slow-cooking pot. In small mixing bowl, combine undiluted soup with wine and basil. Pour over meat. Cover and cook on low for 8 to 10 hours. Sprinkle with parsley. Slice meat; serve with sauce ladled over meat. (Sauce may be thickened with flour dissolved in a small amount of water, if desired.) Makes 6 to 8 servings.

FAVORITE POT ROAST

3 to 4-lb. beef rump or
chuck roast
1 tsp. salt
½ tsp. seasoned salt
¼ tsp. seasoned pepper

¼ tsp. paprika
1 tbs. instant minced
onion
1 cup beef bouillon

Rub all sides of meat with salt, seasoned salt, seasoned, pepper, and paprika. In slow-cooking pot, combine seasoned beef with onion and bouillon. Cover and cook on low 8 to 10 hours or until meat is tender. Remove from pot; slice. Makes 6 to 8 servings. If gravy is preferred, thicken juices with flour dissolved in a small amount of water after removing meat from pot. If desired, vegetables such as potatoes, carrots, small white onions, celery, or turnips may be added with bouillon and cooked the same time as meat.

SPICY WINE POT ROAST

3 to 4-lb. beef pot roast
Salt and pepper
1 small onion, chopped
1 (¾-oz.) package brown
  gravy mix
1 cup water
¼ cup catsup

¼ cup dry red wine
2 tsp. Dijon-style
  mustard
1 tsp. Worcestershire
  sauce
⅛ tsp. garlic powder

Sprinkle meat with salt and pepper; place in slow-cooking pot. Combine remaining ingredients; pour over meat. Cover and cook on low 8 to 10 hours. Remove meat and slice. If desired thicken sauce with flour dissolved in a small amount of water, and serve over meat. Makes 6 to 7 servings.

DILLED POT ROAST

3 to 3½-lb. beef pot roast
1 tsp. salt
¼ tsp. pepper
1 tsp. dill weed
¼ cup water

1 tbs. vinegar
3 tbs. flour
1 tsp. dill weed
1 cup dairy sour cream

Sprinkle both sides of meat with salt, pepper, and 1 tsp. dill. Place in slow-cooking pot. Add water and vinegar. Cover and cook on low for 7 to 9 hours or until tender. Remove meat from pot. Turn control to high. Dissolve flour in small amount of cold water; stir into meat drippings. Stir in additional 1 tsp. dill. Cook on high about 10 minutes or until slightly thick. Stir in sour cream; turn off heat. Slice meat; serve with sauce. Makes 6 to 7 servings.

CORNED BEEF

3 to 4-lb. corned beef
  brisket
Water
½ cup chopped onion

2 garlic cloves, minced
2 bay leaves
1 head cabbage, cut into
  wedges (optional)

Place corned beef in slow-cooking pot. Barely cover with water. Add onion, garlic, and bay leaves. Cover and cook on low for 10 to 12 hours. Makes 6 to 8 servings.

If cabbage is desired, lift cooked corned beef out of pot, turn control to high, and drop wedges of cabbage into corned beef broth. Cover and cook 20 to 30 minutes or until cabbage is done.

SPICED BEEF TONGUE

1 (3 to 4-lb.) beef tongue
2 quarts water
6 whole cloves
6 whole black
  peppercorns

2 tsp. salt
4 bay leaves
¼ cup vinegar

Combine all ingredients in slow-cooking pot. Cover and cook on low for 10 to 12 hours or until tender. Remove from pot; drain. Cool slightly; remove skin with sharp knife. Serve hot or cold. Slice thinly and serve plain, or with horseradish or mustard sauce. It makes delicious sandwiches when served cold. Makes 8 to 10 servings.

GLAZED CORNED BEEF

3½ to 4-lbs. corned beef   1½ tsp. horseradish
Water   2 tbs. red wine vinegar
2 tbs. prepared mustard   ¼ cup molasses

In slow-cooking pot, cover corned beef with water.
Cover and cook on low for 10 to 12 hours. Drain
cooked corned beef; place on broiler pan or oven-
proof platter. Combine mustard, horseradish, wine
vinegar, and molasses. Brush on all sides of meat.
Brown in 400°F. oven for about 20 minutes or until it
begins to brown; brush with sauce several times while
browning. Makes 6 to 8 servings.

SPICY BRISKET

3 lbs. lean beef brisket   1 stalk celery, chopped
1 tsp. salt   ½ cup chili sauce°
¼ tsp. pepper   1 can beer
1 sliced onion

Place beef in slow-cooking pot. Add salt, pepper,
onion, celery, and chili sauce. Pour beer over. Cover
and cook on low for 8 to 10 hours or until tender. Remove beef from pot; slice. Skim fat off juices; serve
juices with meat. Makes 5 to 6 servings.

°Bottled tomato sauce similar to catsup.

LASAGNE

¾ lb. lean ground beef
½ lb. lean ground pork
1 small onion, chopped
1 clove garlic, minced
1 (16-oz.) can tomatoes, cut up
1 (8-oz.) can tomato sauce
1 beef bouillon cube, crushed
1 tbs. parsley flakes
2 tsp. sugar
½ tsp. salt
½ tsp. crushed basil
1 pt. cottage cheese (16 oz.)
½ cup grated Parmesan cheese
½ tsp. salt
½ tsp. crushed oregano
8 oz. lasagne noodles, cooked and drained
8 oz. mozzarella cheese, sliced

In large skillet or slow-cooking pot with browning unit, cook and stir beef, pork, onion, and garlic. Drain off excess fat. In slow-cooking pot, combine drained beef, pork, onion, and garlic with tomatoes, tomato sauce, bouillon cube, parsley, sugar, ½ tsp. salt, and basil. Cover and cook on low for 6 to 8 hours. Mix cottage cheese, ¼ cup Parmesan cheese, ½ tsp. salt, and oregano. In 13 x 9-inch pan, layer half the cooked noodles, sauce, mozzarella cheese, and cottage cheese mixture; repeat, reserving enough sauce for layer on top. Sprinkle with ¼ cup grated Parmesan cheese. Bake in 350°F. oven for 45 minutes. Makes 8 to 10 servings.

SMOKY BRISKET

3 to 4 lbs. lean beef
  brisket
1 tbs. smoke-flavored salt
2 medium onions, sliced
1 tsp. celery seed

1 tbs. mustard seed
½ tsp. pepper
1 (12-oz.) bottle chili
  sauce

Sprinkle both sides of meat with smoke-flavored salt. Arrange onion slices in bottom of slow-cooking pot. Top with meat. Combine celery seed, mustard seed, pepper, and chili sauce. Pour over meat. Cover and cook on low for 10 to 12 hours or until tender. Makes 8 to 10 servings.

FONDUE ITALIANO

1 lb. lean ground beef
1 envelope spaghetti
  sauce mix
2 (15-oz.) cans tomato
  sauce
1 lb. sharp cheddar
  cheese, shredded

8 oz. mozzarella cheese,
  shredded
2 tbs. cornstarch
½ cup dry red wine

In skillet or slow-cooking pot with browning unit, cook beef until crumbly; pour off excess fat. In slow-cooking pot, combine beef with dry spaghetti sauce mix, tomato sauce, cheddar and mozzarella cheeses. Cover and cook on low 2 hours. Dissolve cornstarch in wine. Turn control to high. Add dissolved cornstarch. Heat on high for 10 to 15 minutes. Dip chunks of Italian bread into fondue while keeping mixture hot in slow-cooking pot. May be used as a hearty hot dip or as a main dish served with a salad after the game or theater. Makes 6 to 8 servings.

ITALIAN POT ROAST

3 to 4-lb. beef chuck
  roast
Salt and pepper

1 (1½-oz.) package
  spaghetti sauce mix
2 tomatoes, chopped

Sprinkle meat with salt and pepper and then dry spaghetti seasoning mix. Place in slow-cooking pot. Top with chopped tomatoes. Cover and cook on low for 7 to 9 hours or until meat is tender. Slice and serve on hot spaghetti; spoon sauce over all. Makes 6 to 7 servings.

BEEFBURGER STROGANOFF

1½ lbs. lean ground beef
3 slices bacon, diced
1 small onion
2 tbs. flour
¼ tsp. paprika
1 tsp. salt
1 (10¾-oz.) can

condensed cream of
  mushroom soup
2 tbs. dry red wine
1 cup dairy sour cream
6 to 8 hamburger buns,
  toasted and buttered

In large skillet or slow-cooking pot with browning unit, brown beef and bacon until red color disappears. Drain. In slow-cooking pot, mix together drained beef, bacon, onion, flour, paprika and salt. Stir in undiluted soup and wine. Cover pot and cook on low 4 to 5 hours. Stir in sour cream. Spoon mixture over toasted buns. For an easy-on-the-cook meal, serve with fresh vegetable relishes and potato chips. Makes 6 to 8 servings.

ITALIAN MEAT BALL STEW

1½ lbs. lean ground beef
½ cup fine bread crumbs
2 beaten eggs
¼ cup milk
2 tbs. grated Parmesan
    cheese
1 tsp. salt
⅛ tsp. garlic salt
¼ tsp. pepper
2 carrots, peeled and cut
    into 1-inch slices

1 (6-oz.) can tomato paste
1 cup water
1 cup beef bouillon
½ tsp. oregano
1 tsp. seasoned salt
½ tsp. basil
1 (10-oz.) package frozen
    Italian-style vegetables,
    partially thawed

Combine beef with bread crumbs, eggs, milk, cheese, salt, garlic salt, and pepper. Form into 2-inch balls. Drop carrots in bottom of slow-cooking pot. Arrange meat balls over carrots. Combine tomato paste with water, bouillon, oregano, seasoned salt, and basil. Pour over meat. Cover and cook on low for 4 to 6 hours. Turn to high. Add Italian vegetables. Cover and cook on high for 15 to 20 minutes or until vegetables are tender. Makes 6 servings.

Italian Meat Ball Stew
Courtesy California Beef Council

Spaghetti Sauce with Meatballs
Photo: Theodore R. Sills. Courtesy National Macaroni Institute

FESTIVE MEAT BALLS

1½ lbs. lean ground beef
1 (4½-oz.) can deviled
   ham
⅔ cup evaporated milk
2 eggs, beaten slightly
1 tbs. grated onion
2 cups soft bread crumbs
½ tsp. salt

¼ tsp. allspice
¼ tsp. pepper
¼ cup flour
¼ cup water
1 tbs. catsup
1 tsp. dill weed
1 cup dairy sour cream

Combine beef and ham with milk, eggs, onion, bread crumbs, salt, allspice, and pepper. Shape into meat balls about 2 inches in diameter. (If desired, meat balls may be smaller.) Carefully arrange meat balls in slow-cooking pot. Cover and cook on low for 2½ to 3½ hours. Turn control to high. Stir in flour that has been dissolved in ¼ cup water. Add catsup and dill weed. Cook on high for 15 to 20 minutes or until slightly thickened. Turn heat off; stir in sour cream. Makes 5 to 7 servings.

SPAGHETTI SAUCE

1 lb. lean ground beef
1 large onion, chopped
1 clove garlic, minced
2 (1-lb.) cans tomatoes,
   cut up
1 (8-oz.) can tomato sauce
1 (12-oz.) can tomato
   paste

1 cup beef bouillon
2 tbs. minced parsley
1 tbs. brown sugar
1 tsp. dried oregano
   leaves
1 tsp. dried basil leaves
1 tsp. salt
¼ tsp. pepper

In large skillet or slow-cooking pot with browning unit, crumble meat with onion and garlic. Break up pieces of meat with fork and cook until it loses its red color. Drain off excess fat. In slow-cooking pot, combine browned meat, onions, and garlic with remaining ingredients. Cover and cook on low for 6 to 8 hours. Serve over hot spaghetti. May be made ahead of time and frozen. Makes 6 to 8 servings.

HAMBURGER SOUP

1 lb. lean ground beef
¼ tsp. pepper
¼ tsp. oregano
¼ tsp. basil
¼ tsp. seasoned salt
1 envelope onion soup
  mix
3 cups boiling water

1 (8-oz.) can tomato sauce
1 tbs. soy sauce
1 cup sliced celery
1 cup sliced carrots
1 cup macaroni, cooked
  and drained
¼ cup grated Parmesan
  cheese

Crumble beef into slow-cooking pot. Add pepper, oregano, basil, seasoned salt, and dry soup mix. Stir in water, tomato sauce and soy sauce; then add celery and carrots. Cover and cook on low for 6 to 8 hours. Turn control to high. Add cooked macaroni and Parmesan cheese. Cover and cook on high for 10 to 15 minutes. Makes 5 to 6 servings.

CLARA'S BEEF & POTATOES

2 lbs. lean ground beef
1 tsp. salt
½ tsp. pepper
¼ cup finely chopped
  onion

1 can condensed tomato
  soup
5 to 6 medium potatoes
1 cup light cream

In large skillet or slow-cooking pot with browning unit, brown beef; break up large chunks with fork. Pour off excess fat. In small bowl, mix together salt, pepper, onion, and undiluted soup. Peel and slice potatoes. In slow-cooking pot, arrange alternate layers of potatoes and meat (with potatoes on bottom). Pour soup mixture over. Cover and cook on low for 4 to 6 hours. Turn control to high. Pour cream over all; cover and cook on high for 15 to 20 minutes. Makes 6 servings.

CHEESY MEAT LOAF

16 to 18 round cheese
crackers
1 small onion, finely
chopped
2 tbs. minced green
pepper

¼ cup chili sauce*
½ cup milk
2 eggs, slightly beaten
¾ tsp. salt
⅛ tsp. pepper
1½ lbs. lean ground beef

Crush crackers with rolling pin or blender until crumbled. In mixing bowl, combine crumbs with onion, green pepper, chili sauce, milk, eggs, salt, and pepper. Mix in ground beef. Form into 6- or 7-inch round loaf. Place in slow-cooking pot. Cover and cook on low for 6 to 8 hours or until done. Makes 6 to 8 servings.

*Bottled tomato sauce similar to catsup.

ITALIAN BEEF & POTATO CASSEROLE

1 lb. lean ground beef
1 (5½-oz.) pkg. scalloped
potatoes
1 (16-oz.) can tomatoes
1 (10½-oz.) can pizza
sauce
½ cup water
½ tsp. salt

½ tsp. oregano leaves
¼ tsp. basil leaves
⅛ tsp. garlic powder
1 cup mozzarella cheese,
cut into small cubes
¼ cup grated Parmesan
cheese

In skillet or slow-cooking pot with browning unit, brown meat until crumbly; drain off fat. In slow-cooking pot, combine beef with dry sauce mix from package of scalloped potatoes, tomatoes, pizza sauce, water, salt, oregano, basil and garlic powder. Stir in dry potato slices. Cover and cook on low 4 to 5 hours. Turn control to high. Stir in cubes of mozzarella cheese. Top with Parmesan cheese. Cover and cook on high for 10 to 15 minutes. Makes 4 to 6 servings.

STUFFED GREEN PEPPERS

5 to 6 green peppers
½ lb. lean ground beef
¼ cup finely chopped
 onion
1 tbs. chopped pimiento
1 tsp. salt
1 (12-oz.) can whole
 kernel corn, drained

1 tbs. Worcestershire
 sauce
1 tsp. prepared mustard
1 (10¾-oz.) can
 condensed cream of
 tomato soup

Cut a slice off top of each pepper. Remove core, seeds, and white membrane. In small bowl, combine beef, onion, pimiento, salt, and corn. Spoon into peppers. Stand peppers up in slow-cooking pot. Add Worcestershire sauce and mustard to soup. Pour over peppers. Cover pot; cook on low 8 to 10 hours. Makes 5 to 6 servings.

FAMILY FAVORITE MEAT LOAF

2 beaten eggs
¾ cup milk
⅔ cup fine dry bread
 crumbs

2 tbs. grated onion
1 tsp. salt
½ tsp. ground sage
1½ lbs. ground beef

Sauce:

¼ cup catsup
2 tbs. brown sugar

1 tsp. dry mustard
¼ tsp. ground nutmeg

Combine eggs with milk, bread crumbs, onion, salt, sage, and meat. Mix well and shape into 9 x 5-inch rectangle or oval, or about 6-inch round. Carefully place in slow-cooking pot. Cook on low for 5 to 6 hours. Combine sauce ingredients in small bowl; pour over meat. Cover and cook on high 15 minutes longer. Slice and serve while hot or use cold slices for sandwiches. Makes 6 servings.

SHORT-CUT CHILI CON CARNE

1 lb. lean ground beef
1 small onion, chopped
1 tsp. salt
1 to 2 tsp. chili powder
1 bay leaf
1 tsp. Worcestershire
 sauce

2 (8-oz.) cans tomato
 sauce
2 (16-oz.) cans kidney
 beans, drained

In skillet or slow-cooking pot with browning unit, break up beef with fork and cook until lightly browned. Pour off excess fat. In slow-cooking pot, combine meat with onion, salt, chili powder, bay leaf, Worcestershire sauce, tomato sauce, and kidney beans. Cover and cook on high for 2 to 3 hours. Remove bay leaf. Makes 6 to 7 servings.

Short-Cut Chili Con Carne
Courtesy California Dry Bean Advisory Board

OTHER MEATS

When it comes to a choice of meats for your pot, the sky is the limit. Use your slow-cooking pot as an excuse for trying some of those meats you've seen at the market and always intended to buy. Or, use it for variations of old favorites. This way you can add new variety to your menus without wiping out the budget!

Be sure to check the meat at the minimum suggested cooking time. Let it cook longer if necessary to suit your own taste buds. With a little experience you will develop a "feel" for the time needed for the exact degree of done-ness you like.

Meat recipes combined with vegetables will keep your meat-hungry family happy while allowing you to stay out of the kitchen until the last few minutes before dinner. Some larger roasts are designed to fit into 4½-quart and larger cookers. You may want to use a meat thermometer with these just as you would when cooking in the oven. If yours is a 3½-quart or smaller pot, use a small size roast and/or have the butcher remove any bones and tie the meat to make it more compact. Remember: Smaller roasts take slightly less cooking time.

You will have more meat juices when you finish than you get with other cooking methods. Make the most of the wonderful flavor these juices contain by spooning them over slices of the meat, or thickening them with dissolved flour or cornstarch. Pass the gravy to serve over rice, potatoes or noodles.

Pork—To brown or not to brown—that is the question. It's a good idea to brown spareribs before cooking them in a slow-cooking pot. Lightly brown them in the oven and drain the excess fat before adding sauce and vegetables. If pork steaks and chops are fairly lean, either brown them, or just trim the excess fat off the edges.

Lamb—The same principle applies to lamb. If there is fat, trim off the excess or brown it and drain off the fat before placing it in your slow-cooking pot. You may want to pour off the fat at least once during the cooking process.

GOURMET LEG OF LAMB

1 (5 to 6-lb.) leg of lamb*	2 tbs. peppercorns,
1 clove garlic	cracked
¼ cup Kosher or coarse	¼ cup cognac or brandy
salt	2 cups dry red wine

Trim excess fat from lamb. Cut garlic clove into 4 to
6 slices. Using a paring knife, make enough small slits
to insert slivers of garlic into various parts of meat.
Sprinkle coarse salt and pepper over all sides of lamb.
Place in large bowl; pour cognac or brandy over it.
Refrigerate several hours or overnight, brushing with
cognac or brandy and turning meat several times.
Drain meat and put it and red wine in slow-cooking
pot. Cover and cook on low 10 to 12 hours or until
meat is done. If possible, turn roast in pot once during
cooking. Makes 8 to 10 servings.

*This recipe designed for a 4½ quart or larger slow-
cooking pot. Have your butcher bone the leg of lamb
to fit into a smaller pot.

HERBED LEG OF LAMB

4½ to 5½-lb. leg of
  lamb°
1 clove garlic, peeled
  and halved
1 tbs. dry mustard
1 tsp. salt

⅛ tsp. pepper
½ tsp. thyme leaves
¼ tsp. crushed rosemary
  leaves
1 tbs. lemon juice
¼ cup flour

Rub all surfaces of lamb with garlic. Mix mustard with
salt, pepper, thyme, rosemary and lemon juice. Spread
and pat herb mixture on surface of roast. Place roast
on metal rack in slow-cooking pot. Cover pot and cook
on low for 10 to 12 hours or until tender. Remove meat
to platter. Skim off excess fat from juices. Turn control to high. Dissolve flour in small amount of cold
water. Stir into juices in pot. Cook on high for 15 to 20
minutes. Serve herbed sauce with meat. Makes 8 to
10 servings.

°This recipe designed for a 4½ quart or larger slow-
cooking pot. If you have a smaller pot, ask the butcher
to bone the leg of lamb or buy a smaller one.

SPICY LAMB SHANKS

4 to 5 lamb shanks°
1 tsp. salt
¼ tsp. pepper
1 cup dried apricots
1 cup pitted prunes
1 cup water

2 tbs. vinegar
⅓ cup sugar
½ tsp. ground allspice
½ tsp. ground cinnamon
¼ tsp. ground cloves

Coat lamb shanks with salt and pepper. Place in slow-
cooking pot. Add apricots and prunes. Combine water
and vinegar with sugar, allspice, cinnamon, and cloves.
Pour over fruits and meat. Cover and cook on low for
7 to 9 hours or until meat is tender. Makes 4 to 5
servings.

°Four lamb shanks fit into 3½ qt. slow-cooking pot;
a larger pot is needed for more than 4 shanks.

IRISH LAMB STEW

1½ lbs. lamb, cut into
  2-inch cubes
1 tbs. shortening
2 medium onions,
  chopped
4 cups beef broth
3 medium potatoes,
  peeled and thinly sliced
½ tsp. salt

¼ tsp. pepper
¼ tsp. celery seed
¼ tsp. marjoram leaves,
  crushed
⅛ tsp. thyme leaves,
  crushed
1 (10-oz.) package frozen
  peas, partially thawed
6 tbs. flour

In large skillet or slow-cooking pot with browning unit, brown meat in shortening. Combine browned meat in slow-cooking pot with remaining ingredients except peas and flour. Cover and cook on low for 8 to 10 hours or until meat and potatoes are done. Add peas; then flour dissolved in ½ cup cold water. Turn control to high; cover and cook on high 15 to 20 minutes. Makes 5 to 6 servings.

FRUITED PORK CHOPS

4 lean pork chops
½ tsp. salt
Dash of pepper
1 tbs. prepared mustard
2 tbs. wine vinegar

⅛ tsp. dried dill weed
1 (17-oz.) can fruit
  cocktail
2 tbs. cornstarch
2 tbs. cold water

Sprinkle chops with salt and pepper. Place in slow-cooking pot. Combine mustard, vinegar and dill. Drain fruit cocktail; add ½ cup syrup from fruit to mustard mixture. Pour over chops in pot. Cover pot and cook on low for 4 to 6 hours or until meat is tender. Remove chops and turn control to high. Dissolve cornstarch in water; stir into pot. Add drained fruit cocktail, cover and cook on high for 10 to 15 minutes. Spoon fruit sauce over chops. Makes 4 servings.

Fruited Pork Chops
Courtesy Cling Peach Advisory Board

AUTUMN PORK CHOPS

6 pork chops
2 medium acorn squash,
  unpeeled
¾ tsp. salt
2 tbs. melted butter or
  margarine

¾ cup brown sugar,
  packed
¾ tsp. brown bouquet
  sauce
1 tbs. orange juice
½ tsp. grated orange peel

Trim excess fat from chops. Cut each squash into 4 to
5 crosswise slices; remove seeds. Arrange 3 chops on
bottom of slow-cooking pot. Place all squash slices on
top; then another layer of remaining 3 chops. Combine salt, butter, sugar, bouquet sauce, orange juice,
and orange peel. Spoon over chops. Cover and cook
on low for 4 to 6 hours or until done. Serve one or two
slices of squash with each pork chop. Makes 6 servings.

GOLDEN GLOW PORK CHOPS

5 to 6 pork chops
¼ cup brown sugar
½ tsp. ground cinnamon
¼ tsp. ground cloves
1 (8-oz.) can tomato sauce

1 (29-oz.) can cling peach
  halves
¼ cup vinegar
Salt and pepper

Lightly brown pork chops on both sides in large skillet
or slow-cooking pot with browning unit. Pour off excess fat. Combine brown sugar, cinnamon, cloves,
tomato sauce, ¼ cup syrup from peaches, and vinegar.
Sprinkle chops with salt and pepper. Arrange chops in
slow-cooking pot. Place drained peach halves on top.
Pour tomato mixture over all. Cover and cook on low
for 4 to 6 hours. Makes 5 to 6 servings.

CORN-STUFFED PORK CHOPS

5 to 6 pork chops, 1 to 2
  inches thick
1 (7-oz.) can whole kernel
  corn, not drained
1 cup soft bread crumbs
1 tbs. instant minced
  onion

2 tbs. minced green
  pepper
1 tsp. salt
½ tsp. sage

Have butcher cut a pocket or with a sharp knife cut a
horizontal slit in side of each chop forming a pocket
for stuffing. Mix undrained corn, bread crumbs, onion,
pepper, salt, and sage. Spoon corn mixture into slits.
Close with toothpicks or small skewers. Place on metal
rack or trivet in slow-cooking pot. Cover and cook on
low for 6 to 8 hours. Especially good with fruit salad
and lemon-buttered broccoli. Makes 5 to 6 servings.

RATHSKELLER PORK

4 to 5 pork steaks, about
  ¾ inch thick
1 tbs. salad oil
1 (10½-oz.) can
  condensed cream of
  asparagus soup
½ cup chopped green
  onions

1½ tsp. seasoned salt
½ tsp. seasoned pepper
¼ cup water
4 potatoes, sliced
2 cups shredded cabbage
½ cup light cream

In large skillet or slow-cooking pot with browning
unit, brown chops in oil on both sides. Drain off excess fat. Combine undiluted soup with onions, seasoned salt, pepper and water. Arrange alternate layers
of meat, potatoes and cabbage in slow-cooking pot.
Pour soup mixture over. Cover and cook 4 to 6 hours
on low. Turn to high. Add cream; cover and cook on
high for 20 to 30 minutes. Makes 4 to 5 servings.

1/Fill pork chop pockets with stuffing.

2/Place on metal rack or trivet in slow-cooking pot. Brush with mixture of corn syrup and orange peel.

PLANTATION PORK CHOPS

4 double cut loin pork
  chops
2 cups corn bread stuffing
  mix
2 tbs. melted butter or
  margarine
¼ tsp. salt

⅓ cup orange juice
1 tbs. finely chopped
  pecans
Salt and pepper
¼ cup light corn syrup
½ tsp. grated orange peel

Have butcher cut a pocket or with a sharp knife cut a horizontal slit in side of each chop forming a pocket for stuffing. Combine stuffing with butter, ¼ tsp. salt, orange juice, and pecans. Fill pockets with stuffing. Sprinkle chops with salt and pepper. Place on metal rack in slow-cooking pot. Brush with mixture of corn syrup and orange peel. Cover and cook on low for 6 to 8 hours. Uncover; turn control to high and brush with sauce again. Cook on high for 15 to 20 minutes. Makes 4 servings.

NORTH-OF-THE-BORDER POZOLE

4 pork steaks
Salt and pepper
1 (14½-oz.) can hominy,
  drained

1 small onion, chopped
1 (4-oz.) can diced green
  chili peppers, drained
1 tsp. chili powder

Trim fat off pork steaks; sprinkle with salt and pepper. Combine hominy with onion, chili peppers, and chili powder in bottom of slow-cooking pot. Arrange pork steaks over hominy. Cover and cook on low for 4 to 6 hours. Makes 4 servings.

CRANBERRY PORK ROAST

3 to 4-lb. pork roast°
Salt and pepper
1 cup ground or finely
  chopped cranberries

¼ cup honey
1 tsp. grated orange peel
⅛ tsp. ground cloves
⅛ tsp. ground nutmeg

Sprinkle roast with salt and pepper. Place in slow-cooking pot. Combine remaining ingredients; pour over roast. Cover and cook on low for 8 to 10 hours. Makes 6 to 8 servings.

°Boneless or pork loin roast may be used.

HERBED PORK ROAST

1 (4 to 7-lb.) fresh ham
  or pork leg°
2 cups water
1 tsp. salt
1 tsp. thyme, crumbled

1 tsp. ground sage
1 tsp. grated lemon peel
1 tbs. lemon juice
1 clove garlic

Remove skin and excess fat from pork. Place in large bowl. Pour water over; add remaining ingredients. Cover and refrigerate several hours or overnight. Turn meat two or three times if possible. Transfer meat and marinade to slow-cooking pot. Cover and cook on low for 10 to 12 hours or until meat is done. If possible, turn meat in pot once during cooking. Drain and slice. Makes 8 servings.

°The larger roast fits a 4½ quart or larger slow-cooking pot. If you have a smaller slow-cooking pot, have the butcher bone the roast or buy a smaller one.

INDONESIAN PORK

1 (4 to 5-lb.) pork roast
Salt and pepper
1 cup hot water
¼ cup molasses

¼ cup prepared mustard
¼ cup vinegar
¼ cup orange marmalade
¼ tsp. ground ginger

Place metal rack or trivet in bottom of slow-cooking pot. Sprinkle pork roast with salt and pepper; put on trivet in pot. Pour hot water around pork roast. Cover and cook on low for 8 to 10 hours or until done. Remove meat from pot. Place on broiler pan or ovenproof platter. Combine molasses, mustard, vinegar, marmalade, and ginger. Brush over cooked pork. Brown in 400°F. oven for 30 minutes, brushing several times with sauce. Makes 6 to 8 servings.

SWEET-SOUR SPARERIBS

3 to 4 lbs. spareribs
Salt and pepper
1 cup chicken bouillon
¼ cup brown sugar
¼ cup vinegar
1 tbs. soy sauce
1 small onion, thinly
sliced

2 tbs. cornstarch
1 (11-oz.) can mandarin
oranges, drained
1 medium green pepper,
cut into chunks

Cut spareribs into serving-size pieces. Sprinkle with salt and pepper. Place on rack in shallow baking pan. Roast in 400°F. oven for 15 minutes. Turn and brown other side. Drain fat and put ribs in slow-cooking pot. Combine bouillon with brown sugar, vinegar, and soy sauce. Pour over ribs in pot. Cover and cook on low for 6 to 8 hours. Turn control to high. Add onion. Dissolve cornstarch in small amount of cold water; stir into pot. Cover and cook on high another 10 to 15 minutes or until slightly thickened. Stir in oranges and green pepper. Cover and cook 5 minutes. Serve over cooked rice or crisp Chinese noodles. Makes 4 to 6 servings.

CHINESE STYLE COUNTRY RIBS

¼ cup soy sauce
¼ cup orange marmalade
2 tbs. catsup

1 clove garlic, crushed
3 to 4 lbs. country-style
   spareribs*

Combine soy sauce, marmalade, catsup, and garlic.
Brush on both sides of ribs. Place in slow-cooking pot.
Pour remaining sauce over all. Cover and cook on low
for 8 to 10 hours. Makes 4 to 6 servings.

*Also known as farm-style ribs. Regular spareribs may
be substituted.

SOY-GLAZED SPARERIBS

4 to 5 lbs. spareribs, cut
   into two-rib pieces
Salt and pepper
½ cup pineapple juice
2 tbs. garlic-flavored wine
   vinegar
¼ cup dry white wine

2 tbs. soy sauce
2 tbs. honey
½ cup chicken broth or
   bouillon
2 tbs. cornstarch
3 tbs. cold water

Place spareribs on rack in shallow baking pan. Brown
in 400°F. oven for 30 minutes, turning ribs once. Remove from oven; pour off fat. Sprinkle ribs with salt
and pepper. Place in slow-cooking pot. Combine remaining ingredients except cornstarch and water; pour
over ribs. Cover and cook on low 7 to 9 hours. Turn
control to high. Dissolve cornstarch in 3 tbs. cold water.
Stir into rib mixture. Cook 10 to 15 minutes or until
slightly thickened. Makes 5 to 6 servings.

BUCK'S COUNTY SPARERIBS

2½ to 3 lbs. spareribs
1 tsp. salt
¼ tsp. pepper
1 (1-lb.) can sauerkraut,
drained

1 apple, cored and diced
(with peel)
1 tbs. sugar

Cut spareribs into serving-size pieces. Sprinkle with salt and pepper. Place on rack in baking pan. Brown in 400°F. oven for 15 minutes; turn and brown on other side (about 10 or 15 minutes). Pour off drippings. Spoon sauerkraut into bottom of slow-cooking pot. Top with apple, sprinkle sugar over the apple, and put the ribs on top. Cover pot and cook on low for 6 to 8 hours or until meat is tender. Makes 4 servings.

BARBECUED SPARERIBS

4 to 5 lbs. spareribs, cut
into two-rib pieces
½ cup catsup
2 tbs. brown sugar
½ cup bottled steak
sauce

2 tbs. vinegar
¼ tsp. salt
½ tsp. hickory smoke salt
1 tsp. instant minced
onion

Place spareribs on rack in baking pan. Brown in 400°F. oven for 15 minutes; turn and brown on other side for 10 or 15 minutes. Drain fat and put ribs in slow-cooking pot. Combine remaining ingredients; pour over ribs. Cover and cook on low 6 to 8 hours. Makes 5 to 6 servings.

ALL-PURPOSE BARBECUE SAUCE

1 cup catsup
1 tbs. Worcestershire
    sauce
2 or 3 drops bottled hot
    pepper sauce
1 cup water

¼ cup vinegar
1 tbs. brown sugar
1 tsp. salt
1 tsp. celery seed
1 tbs. instant minced
    onion

Combine ingredients in slow-cooking pot. Cover and cook on low 2 to 3 hours. Makes 2 to 2¼ cups sauce. Good on spareribs, chicken, pork chops, sliced roast beef.

CROCKERY HAM

5 to 7-lb. cooked ham
    (with or without bone,
    butt or shank half)*
Whole cloves

½ cup currant jelly
1 tbs. vinegar
½ tsp. dry mustard
¼ tsp. ground cinnamon

Place ham on metal rack or trivet in slow-cooking pot. Cover and cook on low 5 to 6 hours. Remove ham. Pour off juices; remove rind. Score ham; stud with whole cloves. In small saucepan, melt jelly with remaining ingredients. Remove metal rack or trivet. Return meat to slow-cooking pot. Spoon sauce over ham. Cover pot and cook on high for 20 to 30 minutes, brushing with sauce at least once (several times if possible). Makes 8 to 10 servings.

* The larger cuts of ham fit in a 4½ quart or larger slow-cooking pot. If you own a smaller pot, substitute a boneless ham.

HAM AND CHICKEN PIE

1 (10¾-oz.) can
condensed cream of
mushroom soup
⅛ tsp. marjoram
⅛ tsp. thyme
¼ cup chopped onion
½ cup chopped celery
1 (2½-oz.) can
mushrooms, drained

1 cup diced cooked ham
1 cup diced cooked
chicken
1 (10-oz.) package frozen
peas, thawed
1 (8-oz.) package
refrigerator biscuits
Melted butter
1 tbs. sesame seeds

In large bowl, combine soup with marjoram, thyme,
onion, celery, mushrooms, ham, chicken, and peas.
Pour into slow-cooking pot. Cover and cook on low for
5 to 6 hours. Spoon into shallow baking dish.* Arrange
biscuits on top; brush with melted butter; sprinkle
with sesame seeds. Bake in 350°F. oven for 20 to 25
minutes or until biscuits are brown. Makes 4 to 5
servings.

* Ham and chicken mixture may be refrigerated at this
point, then topped with biscuits and baked just before
serving time.

CASSOULET EN POT

½ lb. bulk pork sausage
1 small onion, sliced
1 clove garlic, minced
2 tbs. minced parsley

2 (15-oz.) cans black-eyed
peas, not drained
½ lb. cooked ham, cubed
¼ cup dry white wine

In skillet or slow-cooking pot with browning unit, cook
sausage until lightly browned. Pour off excess fat. In
slow-cooking pot, arrange alternate layers of sausage,
onion, garlic, parsley, black-eyed peas, and ham. Pour
wine over all. Cover and cook on low for 5 to 7 hours.
Mixture is quite soupy, so serve in bowls. To make a
complete meal, add corn muffins and a big green salad.
Makes 6 servings.

KNOCKWURST WITH HOT GERMAN POTATO SALAD

4 large potatoes
1 onion, sliced
1 tsp. salt
Water
4 slices bacon, diced
2 tbs. flour
2 tbs. sugar
1 tsp. dry mustard

1 tsp. salt
¼ tsp. pepper
⅓ cup vinegar
⅔ cup water
½ tsp. celery seeds
4 knockwurst links
1 tbs. finely chopped
  parsley

Peel and slice potatoes. Combine with onion in slow-cooking pot. Sprinkle with 1 tsp. salt. Cover with water. Cover and cook on low for 5 to 6 hours or on high for 2 to 3 hours. Remove from pot; drain thoroughly and return to pot. In the meantime, cook bacon in skillet. Stir in flour, sugar, mustard, 1 tsp. salt, and pepper; mix well. Add vinegar, ⅔ cup water, and celery seeds. Cook several minutes or until thickened. Pour over cooked drained potatoes in slow-cooking pot. Top with knockwurst. Turn control to high. Cover and cook on high for 30 to 40 minutes or until mixture is hot. Sprinkle with parsley. Makes 4 servings.

HOMESTEAD HAM LOAF

1 lb. ground cooked ham
  (about 3 cups)
½ lb. lean bulk sausage
1 cup dry bread crumbs

1 tbs. prepared mustard
1 egg, beaten
1 tsp. grated onion
½ cup milk

Sauce:

¼ cup brown sauce
½ tsp. dry mustard

2 tbs. orange juice

In mixing bowl, combine ham, sausage, bread crumbs, mustard, egg, onion, and milk. Form into round loaf about 6 inches in diameter, or rectangle or oval about 9 x 5 inches. Place in slow-cooking pot. Cover and cook on low for about 7 hours. Combine ingredients for sauce; brush over loaf the last 30 minutes of cooking. Slice and serve hot. Leftover cold slices of loaf make good sandwiches. Makes 6 servings.

KNOCKWURST & CABBAGE

5 to 6 knockwurst links
1 onion, thinly sliced
1 small head cabbage,
  coarsely shredded

½ tsp. salt
1 tsp. caraway seeds
2 cups chicken
  bouillon

Cut knockwurst into 2-inch chunks. In slow-cooking pot, arrange alternate layers of meat* with onions and cabbage. Sprinkle with salt and caraway seeds. Pour bouillon over all. Cover and cook on low 5 to 6 hours or until cabbage is tender. Makes 6 servings.

* If a more chewy texture in the knockwurst is preferred, meat may be added the last hour of cooking.

POULTRY

Nationality favorites from around the world are represented by the variety of poultry dishes you can create in your slow cooker. Elegant *Chicken Breasts, Saltimbocca Style* competes with *Imperial Duckling* and *Stuffed Turkey Breasts* as glamorous company candidates.

While there seems to be an unlimited variation of family favorites, whole chicken, broiler halves or quarters, cut-up chicken parts or cooked chunks of chicken are equally delicious in a slow cooker. Naturally, the larger whole birds require longer cooking time than the bite-size pieces. As a general rule, chicken does not take as long to cook as beef, pork or lamb. Check it for yourself.

Sometimes vegetables take longer to cook than chicken when using carrots, eggplant, celery, or potatoes in a chicken dish. Be sure the vegetables are covered with liquid such as water, bouillon or tomato sauce. Also, you may want to place the vegetables on the bottom of the pot with the chicken on top. This way, the vegetables cook more evenly and should be done about the same time as the chicken.

Duckling requires special attention because of its excess fat. When cooking duck, be sure to stick it with a fork at 2-inch intervals. Place it on a metal rack or trivet in the bottom of your slow cooker so the fat can drip to the bottom. Then pour off the fat at least once during the cooking.

For a change of pace, you'll like the way turkey parts taste when slow-cooked. Turkey legs, thighs, and wings lend themselves especially well to this cooking method. They are tender, juicy and most flavorful. Larger turkey parts fit into 4½-quart or large pots. If you have a 3½-quart pot, buy the smaller parts or remove the bones so the turkey will fit.

Turkey loaf is a shapely new version of the ever-popular family favorite, meat loaf. Try one and you'll have everyone guessing. Shape it in a loaf or oval, depending on the size of your slow cooker.

CHICKEN MARENGO

2½ to 3-lb. frying
  chicken, cut up
1 (1½-oz.) package
  spaghetti sauce mix

½ cup dry white wine
2 fresh tomatoes,
  quartered
¼ lb. fresh mushrooms

Place chicken parts in bottom of slow-cooking pot. Combine dry spaghetti sauce mix with wine; pour over chicken. Cover and cook on low 6 or 7 hours. Turn control to high. Add tomatoes and mushrooms. Cover and cook on high for 30 to 40 minutes or until tomatoes are done. Makes 4 to 5 servings.

MISSION CHICKEN

2 (2½-lb.) broiler-fryers,
  quartered
¼ cup butter
¼ tsp. ground cinnamon
¼ tsp. ground cloves
1 tsp. salt
1 tsp. seasoned salt
1 (6-oz.) can frozen
  orange juice
  concentrate, thawed

½ cup water
2 or 3 drops hot pepper
  sauce
1 cup seedless grapes,
  halved
½ cup slivered, toasted
  almonds

In large skillet or slow-cooking pot with browning unit, brown chicken in butter. Combine cinnamon, cloves, salt, seasoned salt, orange juice concentrate, water, and hot pepper sauce. Pour this mixture over chicken in slow-cooking pot. Cover and cook on low for 4 to 5 hours or until chicken is tender. Stir in grapes. Place chicken in serving dish; sprinkle with almonds. If preferred, pass sauce in separate bowl or thicken with flour dissolved in a small amount of water. Makes 8 servings.

CHICKEN SESAME

1 frying chicken, cut up
¼ cup flour
3 tbs. sesame seeds
½ tsp. salt
¼ tsp. pepper
¼ cup salad oil
1 small onion, chopped
2 stalks celery, chopped
½ cup dry white wine
1 chicken bouillon cube, crumbled
½ tsp. tarragon
¼ cup cornstarch
¼ cup water
1 cup dairy sour cream

Coat chicken with mixture of flour, sesame seeds, salt, and pepper. In large skillet or slow-cooking pot with browning unit, brown chicken in oil. Add onion, celery, wine, bouillon cube, and tarragon. Cover and cook on low 6 to 8 hours. Turn control to high. Remove chicken to warm shallow dish. Dissolve cornstarch in water and stir into pot. Cook on high 15 minutes. Turn heat off; stir in sour cream. Pour sauce over chicken; serve hot. Makes 5 servings. Especially good with hot rice.

CHICKEN KONA

3 to 4 lbs. frying chicken parts or 2 small broilers, quartered
Salt and pepper
½ cup chopped green onion
½ cup soy sauce
¼ cup dry white wine
½ cup water
½ cup honey

Sprinkle chicken with salt and pepper. Place in slow-cooking pot. Combine onions, soy sauce, wine, and water. Pour over chicken. Cover and cook on low for 3 to 4 hours or until chicken is tender. Remove chicken from pot.* Arrange on broiler pan. Brush honey on chicken. Broil until golden brown, brushing with honey several times. Makes 6 to 8 servings.

* Chicken and sauce may be refrigerated and browned at a later time, if desired.

KOWLOON CHICKEN

3 to 3½ lbs. chicken parts
  (or cut-up fryer)
Salt and pepper
¼ tsp. ground ginger
1 clove garlic, minced
1 cup chicken broth or
  bouillon
1 (8½-oz.) can pineapple
  slices

1 (4-oz.) can water
  chestnuts, drained and
  sliced
4 green onions,
  diagonally sliced
¼ cup cornstarch
¼ cup soy sauce
1 tbs. vinegar

Sprinkle chicken with salt and pepper. Place in slow-cooking pot. Combine ginger, garlic, broth and syrup from pineapple. Cut pineapple slices into fourths. Arrange pineapple and water chestnuts over chicken. Pour ginger sauce over all. Cover and cook on low for 3 to 4 hours or until chicken is tender. Add green onions. Dissolve cornstarch in soy sauce and vinegar. Stir into pot. Cover and cook on high for 10 to 15 minutes or until slightly thickened. Serve with crisp Chinese noodles. Makes 5 to 6 servings.

CREOLE CHICKEN

1 broiler-fryer chicken,
  cut up
1 green pepper, chopped
6 green onions, chopped
1 (16-oz.) can tomatoes,
  cut up
1 (6-oz.) can tomato paste
¼ lb. cooked ham, cubed
  (about ¾ cup)

1 tsp. salt
Several drops bottled hot
  pepper sauce
½ lb. smoked or Polish
  sausage, sliced
3 cups cooked rice

In slow-cooking pot, combine chicken, pepper, onions, tomatoes, tomato paste, ham, salt and pepper sauce. Cover and cook on low for 4 to 5 hours. Turn control to high. Add sausage and cooked rice. Cover and cook on high for 15 to 20 minutes. Makes 6 to 7 servings.

CURRIED CHICKEN

1 (2½ to 3½-lb.) chicken
  fryer, cut up
Salt and pepper
1 tbs. curry powder
1 clove garlic, crushed
1 tbs. melted butter
½ cup chicken bouillon

1 tbs. instant minced
  onion
1 (29-oz.) can cling peach
  halves
½ cup pitted prunes
3 tbs. cornstarch
3 tbs. cold water

Sprinkle chicken with salt and pepper. Place in slow-cooking pot. Combine curry with garlic, butter, bouillon and onion. Drain peaches, saving syrup. Add ½ cup peach syrup to curry mixture. Pour curry sauce over chicken. Cover pot and cook on low for 4 to 6 hours. Remove chicken from pot. Turn control to high. Stir in prunes. Dissolve cornstarch in water; stir into sauce in pot. Cover and cook on high for 10 to 15 minutes or until slightly thickened. Add peaches. Serve chicken with sauce. Peanuts, coconut and chutney are ideal accompaniments to this dish. Makes 4 to 5 servings.

ARROZ CON POLLO

1 frying chicken, cut up
1 tsp. salt
¼ tsp. pepper
1 clove garlic, minced
1/16 tsp. saffron powder
3 cups broth or bouillon

2 tbs. dry sherry
1 (16-oz.) can peas,
  drained
½ cup sliced, stuffed
  green olives
2 cups cooked rice

In slow-cooking pot, combine chicken with salt, pepper, garlic and saffron. Pour chicken broth and sherry over chicken. Cover and cook on low for 4 to 6 hours. Drain chicken; save 2 cups of the broth. Turn control to high. In slow-cooking pot, combine chicken, 2 cups broth, peas, olives, and cooked rice. Cover and cook on high another 20 to 30 minutes, or until hot. Makes 4 to 6 servings.

CHICKEN OLÉ

12 tortillas, cut into
6 or 8 pieces each
4 cups coarsely chopped
cooked chicken
or turkey
1 (10¾-oz.) can
condensed cream of
chicken soup
1 (10¾-oz.) can
condensed cream of
mushroom soup
1 (7-oz.) can green chili
salsa
1 cup dairy sour cream
1 tbs. grated onion
1½ cups grated
cheddar cheese

Lightly grease sides and bottom of slow-cooking pot.
Arrange alternate layers of tortillas with chicken and
mixture of undiluted soups, salsa, sour cream, and
onion. Cover and cook on low 4 to 5 hours. Sprinkle
with cheese and cook on low another 15 or 20 minutes.
Serve with orange and avocado salad, plus additional
warm tortillas. Makes 8 servings.

AMERICANIZED CHICKEN CHOP SUEY

2 whole chicken breasts,
skinned, halved, and
boned
1 tsp. salt
1 tsp. minced
crystallized ginger
1 cup sliced celery
1 (5-oz.) can water
chestnuts, drained and
sliced
1 onion, sliced
2 cups chicken bouillon
2 tbs. soy sauce
1 cup sliced mushrooms
1 (1-lb.) can bean sprouts,
drained
Cooked rice
½ cup slivered almonds

Cut chicken into strips about 2 inches long and ½ inch
thick. Place in slow-cooking pot with salt, ginger, celery, water chestnuts, onion, bouillon, and soy sauce.
Cover and cook on low 5 to 6 hours. Turn control to
high. Add mushrooms and bean sprouts. Cover and
cook on high 15 minutes. Serve over hot rice. Sprinkle
with almonds. Serve with extra soy sauce, if desired.
Makes 4 to 6 servings.

NUTTY CHICKEN BREAST

¼ cup peanut butter
2 tbs. chopped peanuts
2 tbs. soy sauce
1 tbs. instant minced
   onion
1 tbs. minced parsley
1 clove garlic, crushed
Several drops red pepper
   sauce
⅛ tsp. ground ginger

4 whole chicken breasts,
   halved, skinned and
   boned
2 tbs. soy sauce
2 tbs. honey
1 tbs. melted butter or
   margarine
1 (10½-oz.) can chicken
   broth
1 tbs. cornstarch

Mix peanut butter, peanuts, 2 tbs. soy sauce, onion,
parsley, garlic, pepper sauce, and ginger. Spread on
inside of each chicken breast. Fold in half; close with
small skewer or a toothpick. Place in slow-cooking pot.
Mix remaining 2 tbs. soy sauce with honey, butter, and
broth; pour over chicken. Cover and cook on low for
4 to 5 hours. Remove chicken from pot. Turn control
to high. Dissolve cornstarch in small amount of cold
water; stir into sauce. Cook on high for about 15 minutes. Makes 8 chicken rolls. Serve with sauce.

BUSY WOMAN'S ROAST CHICKEN

1 (6-oz.) pkg. Stove-Top
  Dressing
1¼ cups water
¼ cup sauterne wine
12 carrots, peeled and
  cut into 2-inch pieces

1 (4 to 5-lb.) roasting
  chicken
Salt and pepper

Prepare dressing according to package directions with 1¼ cups water. Set aside to cool. When cool, stir in sauterne. Meanwhile, in saucepan, cook carrots in small amount of water for 5 minutes. Drain and place in slow-cooking pot. Rinse and dry chicken; stuff with dressing. Place on top of carrots in slow-cooking pot. Sprinkle with salt and pepper. Cover pot and cook on low for 6 to 8 hours or until chicken is tender. If a browner chicken is preferred, place in baking pan in 400° oven for about 15 minutes. Slice chicken; serve with carrots. Makes 6 to 7 servings.

CHICKEN PARMIGIANA

3 whole chicken breasts
  (or 6 halves)
1 egg
1 tsp. salt
¼ tsp. pepper
1 cup dry bread crumbs
½ cup butter

1 small eggplant, cut into
  large slices (about
  ¾-inch thick)
1 (10½-oz.) can pizza
  sauce
6 slices mozzarella cheese
Parmesan cheese

If using whole chicken breasts, cut into halves. In bowl, beat egg, salt, and pepper. Dip chicken into egg. Then coat with crumbs. In large skillet or slow-cooking pot with browning unit, sauté chicken in butter. Arrange eggplant and chicken in pot (place eggplant on bottom or it will not cook completely). Pour pizza sauce over chicken. Cover and cook on low 6 to 8 hours. Add mozzarella cheese; sprinkle Parmesan cheese on top. Cover and cook 15 minutes. Makes 6 servings.

CHICKEN BREASTS, SALTIMBOCCA STYLE

3 whole chicken breasts,
   skinned and boned
6 small slices ham
6 small slices Swiss
   cheese
¼ cup flour
¼ cup grated Parmesan
   cheese

1 tsp. salt
½ tsp. powdered sage
¼ tsp. pepper
⅓ cup salad oil
1 (10½-oz.) can
   condensed cream of
   chicken soup
½ cup dry white wine

Cut each boned chicken breast in half; pound until thin between two sheets of waxed paper or foil. Place slice of ham and cheese on each piece of chicken. Roll up and tuck ends in; secure with small skewer or toothpick. Dip chicken rolls into mixture of flour, Parmesan cheese, salt, sage, and pepper. Save any leftover flour mixture. Chill chicken for at least one hour. In large skillet or pot with browning unit, heat oil and sauté chicken on all sides. Place browned chicken in slow-cooking pot; add soup mixed with wine. Cover and cook on low for 4 to 5 hours. Turn control to high. Thicken with leftover flour dissolved in a small amount of water. Cook on high for 10 minutes. Serve with hot rice. Makes 6 chicken rolls.

CHICKEN TETRAZZINI

1 (2½ to 3-lb.) chicken,
  cut up
1 cup water
½ cup dry white wine
1 medium onion,
  chopped
1 tsp. salt
¼ tsp. thyme
¼ tsp. pepper
2 tbs. minced parsley
⅓ cup butter or
  margarine

⅓ cup flour
½ cup light cream
1 (4-oz.) can mushrooms,
  drained
8 oz. spaghetti, broken
  into 2-inch pieces,
  cooked and drained
½ cup grated Parmesan
  cheese

In slow-cooking pot, combine chicken, water, wine,
onion, salt, thyme, pepper, and parsley. Cover and
cook on low 10 to 12 hours or until chicken is very well
done. Remove chicken. Strain broth into bowl or container. Remove meat from bones. Cut chicken into
slivers and set aside.° Add butter to slow-cooking pot;
turn control to high. Melt butter; stir in flour. Gradually pour in broth, then cream. Cook on high 30 minutes or until bubbly. Stir in cooked chicken, mushrooms, and cooked spaghetti. Cover and cook on high
15 minutes. Sprinkle top with Parmesan cheese. Makes
8 servings.

° Chicken and broth may be cooked the day ahead of
serving and refrigerated at this point. Then, one hour
before serving time, combine with remaining ingredients and complete.

CHICKEN NAPOLI

1 frying chicken, cut up
1 tsp. seasoned salt
¼ cup flour
½ tsp. salt
⅛ tsp. pepper
2 tbs. grated Parmesan
cheese
½ tsp. paprika
1 lb. zucchini, cut into
thin slices
½ cup chicken bouillon
1 (4-oz.) can mushrooms,
drained

Sprinkle chicken with seasoned salt. Combine flour, salt, pepper, cheese, and paprika; coat chicken with mixture. Place zucchini in bottom of slow-cooking pot. Pour bouillon over zucchini. Arrange coated chicken over all. Cover and cook on low for 5 to 6 hours or until tender. Turn control to high. Add mushrooms, cover and cook on high another 10 to 15 minutes. Makes 4 to 6 servings.

CHICKEN CACCIATORA

1 (2½ to 3-lb.) broiler-
fryer chicken, cut-up
¼ cup salad oil
1 onion, chopped
2 (8-oz.) cans tomato
sauce
1 tsp. dried oregano
leaves, crushed
¼ tsp. dried thyme
leaves, crushed
1 tsp. salt
¼ tsp. pepper
1 clove garlic, minced
2 tbs. dry red wine
1 (2-oz.) can sliced
mushrooms, drained
Cooked spaghetti

In large skillet or slow-cooking pot with browning unit, brown chicken in hot oil. Drain. In slow-cooking pot, combine chicken with onion, tomato sauce, oregano, thyme, salt, pepper, garlic and wine. Cover and cook on low for 4 to 5 hours. Stir in drained mushrooms. Spoon over hot cooked spaghetti. Makes 4 to 5 servings.

POACHED CHICKEN

1 stewing chicken (5 to 6 lbs.) or 2 broiler-fryers
Water
1 stalk celery, halved (with leaves)
1 carrot, peeled and halved
1 small onion, halved
1 tsp. salt
3 or 4 sprigs parsley
1 small bay leaf
2 whole cloves
½ tsp. thyme leaves

Sauce:

4 tbs. butter or margarine
¼ cup flour
1 cup chicken broth or bouillon
½ tsp. salt
⅛ tsp. pepper
¼ cup chopped parsley
½ cup heavy cream
2 tbs. butter or margarine

In slow-cooking pot, cover chicken with water. Add celery, carrot, onion, and salt. Tie parsley, bay leaf, cloves, and thyme in small square of cheesecloth. Add to pot. Cover and cook on low for 7 to 9 hours. Melt 4 tbs. butter in medium saucepan. Stir in flour and cook over low heat several minutes. Gradually stir in broth; simmer until smooth. Add salt, pepper, parsley, and cream. Just before serving, beat in remaining 2 tbs. butter, 1 tbs. at a time. Remove chicken from pot; slice and serve with creamy sauce. Makes 5 to 7 servings.

CHICKEN & HERB DUMPLINGS

1 (2½ to 3-lb.) chicken, cut up
1 tsp. salt
¼ tsp. pepper
2 whole cloves
8 to 10 small white onions
1 clove garlic, minced
¼ tsp. powdered marjoram
¼ tsp. powdered thyme
1 bay leaf
½ cup dry white wine
1 cup dairy sour cream
1 cup packaged biscuit mix
1 tbs. chopped parsley
6 tbs. milk

Sprinkle chicken with salt and pepper; place in slow-cooking pot. Insert cloves in one onion. Put all onions in pot. Add garlic, marjoram, thyme, bay leaf, and wine. Cover and cook on low 5 to 6 hours. Remove bay leaf and cloves. Stir in sour cream. Turn control to high. Combine biscuit mix with parsley; stir milk into biscuit mix with fork until well moistened. Drop dumplings from teaspoon around edge of pot. Cover and cook on high for 30 minutes. Makes 5 servings.

ANNE'S CHICKEN

1 frying chicken, cut up
2 tbs. melted butter or margarine
Salt and pepper
2 tbs. dry Italian salad dressing mix
1 (10¾-oz.) can condensed mushroom soup, undiluted
2 (3-oz.) packages cream cheese, cut into cubes
½ cup sauterne or sherry
1 tbs. chopped onion

Wash chicken and pat dry. Brush with butter. Sprinkle with salt and pepper. Place in slow-cooking pot. Sprinkle dry salad mix over. Cover and cook on low for 5 to 6 hours. About ¾ hour before serving, mix soup, cream cheese, wine, and onion in small saucepan. Cook until smooth. Pour over chicken in pot. Cover and cook 30 minutes on low. Serve with sauce. Makes 4 to 5 servings. Serve with rice or noodles.

BRUNSWICK STEW

1 (2½ to 3-lb.) chicken,
cut up
2 qts. water
1 onion, chopped
2 cups cubed cooked ham
3 potatoes, diced
2 (16-oz.) cans tomatoes,
cut up
1 (10-oz.) package frozen

lima beans, partially
thawed
1 (10-oz.) package frozen
whole kernel corn,
partially thawed
2 tsp. salt
½ tsp. seasoned salt
1 tsp. sugar
¼ tsp. pepper

In slow-cooking pot, combine chicken with water, onion, ham, and potatoes. Cook, covered, on low for 4 to 5 hours or until chicken is done. Lift chicken out of pot. Remove meat from bones. Return chicken meat to pot. Add tomatoes, beans, corn, salt, seasoned salt, sugar, and pepper. Turn control to high. Cover and cook on high 1 hour. Serve in large individual bowls. Makes 8 servings.

BARBECUED TURKEY LEGS

4 uncooked turkey
drumsticks*
Salt and pepper
¼ cup molasses
¼ cup vinegar
¼ cup catsup

2 tbs. Worcestershire
sauce
½ tsp. hickory smoke salt
1 tbs. instant minced
onion

Sprinkle turkey with salt and pepper. Place in slow-cooking pot. Combine remaining ingredients; pour over turkey. Cover and cook on low for 5 to 7 hours. If turkey legs are small, serve one thigh or one drumstick per person; if large, slice off cooked meat and serve with sauce. Makes 4 to 6 servings.

* Use 4 thighs, 2 drumsticks and 2 thighs, or 4 drumsticks. Drumsticks may get done first, so check them before thighs. Cooking time on both parts will vary with the size. Use smaller size parts in smaller cooking pot.

SWEET & SOUR TURKEY WINGS

4 uncooked turkey wings
3 cups chicken broth or
  bouillon
½ cup finely chopped
  celery
1 tsp. salt
3 tbs. cornstarch
¼ cup brown sugar

¼ cup vinegar
¼ cup soy sauce
⅓ cup chili sauce*
½ green pepper, cut into
  strips
1 (13½-oz.) can
  pineapple chunks,
  drained

Separate wings at joints and discard tips. In slow-cooking pot, combine wings, broth, celery, and salt. Cover and cook on low for 4 to 6 hours or until tender. Drain, saving 1½ cups broth for sauce.** In large skillet, combine cornstarch, brown sugar, 1½ cups broth, vinegar, soy sauce, and chili sauce. Cook and stir until thick and clear. Stir in green pepper and pineapple; simmer for 2 minutes. Add drained, cooked wings. Bring to simmer. Serve over rice. Makes 4 servings.

* Bottled tomato sauce similar to catsup.
** Wings may be cooked ahead and refrigerated with broth at this point; sweet-sour sauce may be made just before serving.

STUFFED TURKEY BREAST*

¼ cup melted butter
1 small onion, finely chopped
½ cup finely chopped celery
1 (2½-oz.) package bacon croutons
1 cup chicken bouillon
2 tbs. fresh minced parsley
½ tsp. poultry seasoning
1 whole uncooked turkey breast or 2 halves (about 5 lbs.)
Salt and pepper
Cheesecloth (about 24 x 36 inches for each turkey breast)
Dry white wine

Combine butter, onion, celery, croutons, bouillon, parsley, and poultry seasoning. Cut turkey breast in thick slices, from breastbone to rib cage, leaving slices attached to bone. Sprinkle turkey with salt and pepper. Soak cheesecloth in wine. Set turkey on cheesecloth. Stuff bread mixture into slits of turkey. Fold one end of cheesecloth over other to cover meat. Place on metal rack or trivet in slow-cooking pot. Cover pot and cook on low for 7 to 9 hours or until tender. Pour additional wine over turkey during cooking. Remove from pot and take cheesecloth off immediately. If browner breast is preferred, remove from pot and brown in 400°F. oven for 15 to 20 minutes. Let stand 10 minutes. Drippings may be thickened for gravy if desired. Serve each person one or more thick slices of turkey with dressing in between. Makes 8 or 9 servings.

* This recipe designed for 4½ quart or larger slow-cooking pot.

1/Cut turkey breast
in thick slices from
breastbone to rib cage,
leaving slices
attached to bone.

2/Set turkey on
cheesecloth. Stuff
bread mixture
into slits of turkey.

3/Fold one end
of cheesecloth over
other to cover
meat. Place meat on
rack or trivet in
slow-cooking pot.

Lime-Glazed Cornish Hens
Courtesy Cling Peach Advisory Board

RED RAISIN CORNISH HENS

1 (6-oz.) package
stove-top stuffing mix

4 to 5 Cornish hens
Salt and pepper

Sauce:

1 ((10-oz.) jar red currant
jelly
½ cup golden raisins
¼ cup butter or
margarine

2 tsp. lemon juice
¼ tsp. allspice

Mix stuffing according to package directions and stuff
hens. Sprinkle with salt and pepper. Place trivet in
slow-cooking pot. For 3½ quart pot, place hens on
end, neck down. In saucepan, combine jelly, raisins,
butter, lemon juice and allspice. Cook on low heat,
stirring constantly, until blended. Brush some of the
sauce on hens in the pot. (Brush hens once during
cooking, if possible.) Cover slow-cooking pot and cook
on low for 5 to 7 hours. Spoon remaining sauce over
hens at serving time. Makes 4 to 5 servings.

LIME-GLAZED CORNISH HENS

4 to 5 Cornish game hens
1 (8-oz.) package stuffing
mix
¼ cup melted butter

2 tbs. brown sugar
2 tbs. lime juice
2 tbs. dry white wine
2 tsp. soy sauce

Thaw hens, if frozen. Follow directions for stuffing
mix. Spoon stuffing into cavity of each hen. Mix butter
with sugar, lime juice, wine, and soy sauce. Brush hens
with sauce. Place trivet in slow-cooking pot. For 3½
quart pot, place hens on end, neck end down. Cover
and cook on low for 5 to 7 hours. Brush with sauce
once during cooking if possible. Makes 4 to 5 servings.

CRAN-ORANGE TURKEY ROLL

¼ cup sugar
2 tbs. cornstarch
¾ cup orange marmalade
1 cup fresh cranberries, ground or finely chopped

1 (2 to 2½-lb.) frozen turkey roll, partially thawed
Salt and pepper

In small saucepan, blend sugar and cornstarch; stir in marmalade and cranberries. Cook and stir until mixture is bubbly and slightly thickened. Place partially thawed turkey roll in slow-cooking pot. Sprinkle lightly with salt and pepper. Pour sauce over turkey. Cover and cook on low for 9 to 10 hours. (Insert meat thermometer in turkey roll the last 2 or 3 hours; cover and cook until temperature reaches 185°F.) Slice turkey roll; spoon sauce over. Makes 6 servings.

TURKEY LOAF

2 lbs. ground uncooked turkey
1½ cups soft bread crumbs
2 eggs, slightly beaten
1 small onion, minced

1 tsp. prepared horseradish
1 tsp. salt
1 tsp. dry mustard
¼ cup catsup
¼ cup evaporated milk

Combine turkey with remaining ingredients. Form into a 7-inch round loaf. Place in bottom of slow-cooking pot. Cover and cook on low for 5 to 6 hours. Makes 6 to 7 servings. Good served hot with cranberry sauce or sliced cold for sandwiches.

BURGUNDY-BASTED DUCKLING

1 (4 to 5-lb.) ready-to-cook
duckling*
¼ cup Burgundy wine
¼ cup lemon juice
1 tbs. melted butter or
margarine
1 tbs. Worcestershire
sauce

1 clove garlic, minced
1 tsp. salt
1 tsp. dried marjoram,
crushed
¼ tsp. pepper
2 or 3 drops bottled hot
pepper sauce

With a fork, prick skin of duckling all over at approximately two-inch intervals. Place metal rack or trivet
in bottom of slow-cooking pot. Set duckling, breast
side up, in pot. Combine Burgundy, lemon juice, butter, Worcestireshire sauce, garlic, salt, marjoram, pepper, and pepper sauce. Brush about half the sauce over
duckling. Cover and cook on low for 7 to 9 hours. If
possible, remove excess fat, brush duckling with more
sauce, and turn duckling once during cooking. Remove
excess fat again at end of cooking time on low. Then
turn control to high, brush with remaining sauce and
cook a final 30 minutes. If a browner bird is desired,
it may be placed on a broiler pan or heat-proof platter
and browned in 400°F. oven for about 15 or 20 minutes. Makes 4 servings.

* If desired, duckling may be cut into halves or quarters before cooking to fit 3½ quart or smaller cooking
pot.

VEGETABLES

One of the greatest advantages of cooking vegetables in a slow cooker is being able to cook them ahead of time. It is not necessary to watch, stir, or worry about boil overs. You can be doing something else around the house or running errands at the local shopping center. When you return, the vegetables are done. Serve them for dinner or combine with other ingredients in a casserole and brown them in the oven to serve later.

Rules for cooking vegetables vary almost as much as the vegetables themselves. For example, you will discover countless ways to prepare the squash family in your slow cooker. You can stuff acorn squash, glaze banana squash, mash banana squash, and simmer zucchini. You can cook squash in your pot, add other ingredients and finish the dish in the oven.

Carrots, celery, turnips, parsnips and beets take an extra long time to cook in a slow-cooking pot. Strangely enough, *these vegetables take as long or longer to cook than many meats*. Be sure to consider this when combining vegetables with meat.

Recipes for sweet potatoes or yams may be interchanged. Use the one you prefer or whichever is available in your market.

Sweet and white potatoes are delicious when "baked" in a slow-cooking pot. Wash the potatoes but do not actually dry. While still damp, place in slow cooker and cook on low until soft and tender. You cannot use this baking method with all slow cookers. The Use and Care chapter tells which brands you can bake in.

It is wise to turn the control to **HIGH** when you are cooking most vegetables in a slow cooker. Many of them have a tendency to dry out and discolor when left on **LOW** for a long time.

RHINELAND SWEET-SOUR RED CABBAGE

4 slices bacon, diced
¼ cup brown sugar
2 tbs. flour
1 tsp. salt
⅛ tsp. pepper
½ cup water

¼ cup vinegar
1 medium head red
   cabbage, shredded (6
   to 8 cups)
1 small onion, finely
   chopped

Cook bacon in skillet or slow-cooking pot with browning unit. Set bacon aside. Combine 1 tbs. of bacon drippings in slow-cooking pot with sugar, flour, salt, and pepper. Stir in water and vinegar; add cabbage and onion. Cover and cook on low 3 to 4 hours. Spoon into serving bowl; sprinkle cooked bacon on top. Makes 6 to 8 servings.

MOTHER-IN-LAW'S SAUERKRAUT

4 slices bacon, diced
1 (1-lb. 11-oz.) can
   sauerkraut
1 head cabbage, chopped
1 large onion, diced

1 tbs. butter or
   margarine
1 tsp. sugar
½ tsp. salt
⅛ tsp. pepper

In small skillet, cook bacon, saving drippings. In slow-cooking pot, combine sauerkraut, cabbage, onion, butter, sugar, salt, and pepper. Pour cooked bacon and drippings over all. Cover and cook on low for 3 to 5 hours. Makes 8 servings.

ORANGE-GLAZED CARROTS

3 cups thinly sliced
    carrots
2 cups water
¼ tsp. salt

3 tbs. butter or
    margarine
3 tbs. orange marmalade
2 tbs. chopped pecans

Combine carrots, water, and salt in slow-cooking pot.
Cover and cook on high 2 to 3 hours or until carrots are
done. Drain well; stir in remaining ingredients. Cover
and cook on high 20 to 30 minutes. Makes 5 to 6 servings.

CARROTS IN DILLED WINE SAUCE

8 medium carrots, cut
    into small sticks
½ cup chicken bouillon
½ cup dry white wine
½ tsp. dried dill weed
2 tsp. instant minced
    onion

¼ tsp. garlic salt
1 tbs. lemon juice
2 tbs. cornstarch
2 tbs. cold water

Place carrots in slow-cooking pot. Combine bouillon,
wine, dill, onion, garlic salt, and lemon juice. Pour over
carrots. Cover and cook on high 2 to 3 hours. Dissolve
cornstarch in water. Stir into carrot mixture. Cook on
high 10 minutes or until slightly thickened. Makes 6
servings.

CORN PUDDING

3 slightly beaten eggs
2 cups cooked or canned
  whole kernel corn,
  drained
2 cups milk, scalded

1 tbs. instant minced
  onion
1 tbs. melted butter
1 tsp. sugar
1 tsp. salt

Combine ingredients; pour into greased 1½-qt. baking dish.° Cover with foil or lid (do not use plastic). Set metal rack or trivet in bottom of slow-cooking pot. Pour 4 cups hot water in pot. Set baking dish on rack in hot water. Cover pot and cook on high for 2 to 2½ hours or until done. Makes 6 servings.

°1½-qt. baking dish fits into 4½ quart or larger slow-cooking pot.

CORN STUFFING BALLS

½ cup celery with leaves,
  chopped
1 small onion, chopped
1 (17-oz.) can cream-style
  corn
¼ cup water
⅛ tsp. pepper

1 tsp. poultry seasoning
1 (8-oz.) package herb-
  seasoned stuffing mix
2 slightly beaten eggs
¼ cup melted butter or
  margarine

In mixing bowl, combine celery, onion, corn, water, pepper, poultry seasoning, stuffing mix, and eggs. Shape into 7 or 8 balls. Place in slow-cooking pot. Pour butter over. Cover and cook on low for 3 to 4 hours. Serve with broiled meats or roasts, or use as extra dressing with turkey.

TAMALE PUFF*

1 (1-lb.) can cream style
corn
1 (1-lb.) can whole kernel
corn, drained
1 (4-oz.) can chopped
green chilies, drained

1 small onion, finely
chopped
4 eggs
1 (16-oz.) can tamales
½ cup grated cheddar
cheese

In medium mixing bowl, combine cream style and whole kernel corn, chilies and onion. In small bowl, beat eggs until frothy; fold into corn mixture. Spoon corn-egg mixture into 2½-qt. baking dish. Cut tamales in half; arrange on top. Sprinkle with cheese. Cover baking dish with foil. Place metal rack or trivet in bottom of slow-cooking pot. Pour 2 cups hot water in pot. Set filled baking dish on trivet in pot. Cover pot and cook on high for 2½ to 3½ hours. Makes 6 servings.

* This recipe is designed for a 4½ quart or larger slow-cooking pot.

GREEN BEANS PORTUGUESE STYLE

¼ lb. salt pork
2 lbs. fresh green beans
2 medium tomatoes
2 cups beef bouillon

½ tsp. salt
½ tsp. sugar
¼ tsp. pepper

Dice salt pork and spread over bottom of slow-cooking pot. Wash beans. Break each bean into 2 or 3 pieces; place in pot over salt pork. Peel, seed and cube tomatoes; spoon over beans. Add bouillon with salt, sugar, and pepper. Cover and cook on high for 3 to 4 hours or until beans are tender. Drain and serve hot. Makes 8 servings.

TURNIP WHIP

4 turnips, peeled and
    quartered
4 potatoes, peeled and
    quartered
2 tbs. minced onion
1 tsp. salt

Water
¼ cup light cream
2 tbs. soft butter or
    margarine
½ tsp. salt
⅛ tsp. pepper

In slow-cooking pot, combine turnips, potatoes, onion
and 1 tsp. salt. Cover with water. Cover pot and cook
on low for 6 to 8 hours or until vegetables are tender.
Drain well. Mash; add cream, butter, ½ tsp. salt and
pepper. Beat until fluffy. Makes 6 servings.

ORANGE-GLAZED PARSNIPS

8 to 10 medium parsnips
Water
1 tsp. salt
2 tbs. butter or margarine

2 tbs. honey
½ tsp. seasoned salt
¼ cup orange juice
½ tsp. grated orange peel

Wash and peel parsnips. Cut into sticks about ¼-inch
thick. Cover with water in slow-cooking pot; add salt.
Cover and cook on high for 2 to 4 hours or until
tender. Drain. Meanwhile, in saucepan, melt butter,
stir in honey, seasoned salt, orange juice, and peel.
Heat to boiling. Pour over drained parsnips. Makes 5
to 6 servings.

STUFFED POTATOES

5 to 6 large baking
   potatoes
3 tbs. butter
½ cup milk
½ cup dairy sour cream

1 tsp. salt
⅛ tsp. pepper
2 tbs. grated Parmesan
   cheese
Chopped chives

Wash potatoes; drain but do not dry. Place damp potatoes in slow-cooking pot. Cover pot and cook on low for 6 to 8 hours or until tender. Remove from pot. Cut a thick, lengthwise slice from top of each potato. Scoop hot potato pulp into mixing bowl, saving the potato "shell." Add butter, milk, sour cream, salt, and pepper. Beat until fluffy, adding more milk if necessary. Spoon mixture into shells, mounding tops. Sprinkle with cheese. Place in shallow baking pan. Bake in 425°F. oven for 15 minutes or until hot and lightly browned. Top with chopped chives. Makes 5 to 6 servings.

PEACH CHUTNEY

4 cups diced peaches
   (two 29-oz. cans)
1 cup raisins
1 small onion, chopped
1 clove garlic, minced
1 tbs. mustard seed
1 tsp. chopped dried red
   chilies

¼ cup chopped
   crystallized ginger
1 tsp. salt
¾ cup vinegar
½ cup brown sugar

Combine ingredients in slow-cooking pot. Cover and cook on low 4 to 6 hours. Remove lid; turn control to high and cook for 1 or 2 hours. Makes about 4 cups. Serve with curried lamb, shrimp or chicken.

ACORN SQUASH, INDONESIAN

3 acorn squash
Salt and pepper
¼ cup melted butter

⅓ cup chutney*
⅓ cup flake coconut

Cut squash in half; remove seeds. Wash and drain excess water but do not dry. Sprinkle with salt and pepper. Place in slow-cooking pot. Cover and cook on low for 3 to 5 hours or until tender. Remove from pot; set, cut side up, on broiler pan or heat-proof platter. Brush inside of squash with butter. Mix chutney and coconut; spoon into cavity of squash. Bake in 400°F. oven for about 15 minutes or until bubbly. Makes 6 servings.

* Make chutney in slow-cooking pot (see recipe on previous page).

CANDIED BANANA SQUASH*

6 serving-size pieces
  banana squash
¼ cup granulated sugar
¼ cup packed brown
  sugar

¼ cup melted butter
¼ tsp. salt

Remove seeds and membrane from squash. Arrange squash, skin side down, in slow-cooking pot. Cover and cook on low for 5 to 6 hours or until almost done. Combine sugars with butter and salt. Turn control to high. Spoon sauce over squash. Cover and cook on high for 15 to 20 minutes. Makes 6 servings.

* This recipe is designed for a 4½ quart or larger slow-cooking pot.

STUFFED BUTTERNUT SQUASH

3 butternut squash
1 cup hot water
3 tbs. soft butter
¼ tsp. salt
1 tbs. corn syrup

2 tbs. raisins
¼ cup chopped walnuts
¼ cup brown sugar
2 tbs. melted butter

Cut squash in half; remove seeds. Place metal rack or trivet in bottom of slow-cooking pot. Pour in 1 cup hot water. Arrange squash on rack. Cover pot and cook on high 2 to 3 hours or until done. Remove from pot; scrape out pulp down to the skin. Add 3 tbs. butter, salt, and corn syrup to pulp and beat until smooth. Stir in raisins and nuts. Put filling back into shells; place on broiler pan. Combine brown sugar with 2 tbs. melted butter. Drizzle over top of filled squash. Place under broiler several minutes or until top is slightly crusty. Makes 6 servings.

STUFFED PATTYPAN SQUASH

8 to 10 pattypan squash
  (light green summer
  squash)
Water

1 tsp. salt
1 (10-oz.) package frozen
  creamed peas or mixed
  creamed vegetables

In slow-cooking pot, cover squash with water; add salt. Cover and cook on low for 6 to 7 hours or until squash is tender. Drain. Meanwhile, cook peas or vegetables according to package directions. Scoop out squash pulp in center. Fill with hot creamed peas or hot mixed creamed vegetables. Makes 5 to 6 servings.

HERBED SQUASH AU GRATIN

8 to 10 summer squash
(about 2 lbs.)
Water
1 tsp. salt
¼ cup butter or
margarine

2 cups herb-seasoned
croutons
½ cup grated cheddar
cheese

Cut squash into ¼-inch thick crosswise slices. Cover
with water in slow-cooking pot. Add salt. Cover and
cook on low for 3 to 4 hours or until tender. Drain.
Meanwhile, melt butter in small skillet. Stir in croutons; heat until lightly browned. Add cheese. Sprinkle
over well-drained squash. Makes 6 to 8 servings.

SQUASH MEDLEY

8 unpeeled summer
squash (about 1 lb.)
½ tsp. salt
2 small tomatoes,
peeled and chopped
½ small green pepper,
chopped

¼ cup sliced green
onions
1 cup chicken bouillon
4 slices bacon, cooked
and crumbled
¼ cup fine dry bread
crumbs

Thinly slice squash; sprinkle with salt. In slow-cooking
pot, arrange alternate layers of squash with tomatoes,
green pepper, and onions. Pour bouillon over. Top with
bacon, then bread crumbs. Cover pot and cook on
low for 4 to 6 hours. Makes 5 to 6 servings.

DOUBLE SQUASH COMBO

1½ lbs. zucchini
1½ lbs. summer squash
½ tsp. salt
¼ tsp. pepper
⅛ tsp. garlic salt
¼ cup butter or
  margarine

3 tbs. fine dry bread
  crumbs
3 tbs. grated Parmesan
  cheese

Cut both kinds of squash into ½-inch pieces. Put in bottom of slow-cooking pot. Sprinkle with salt, pepper, and garlic salt. Dot with butter; sprinkle with crumbs and cheese. Cover and cook on low for 6 to 7 hours or until tender. Makes 6 to 8 servings.

YAM PUDDING

6 large yams or sweet
  potatoes
¼ cup butter or
  margarine
¼ cup brown sugar

2 tsp. grated lemon peel
1 tbs. lemon juice
½ tsp. salt
⅓ cup brown sugar
½ cup slivered almonds

Wash yams; drain but do not dry. Set in slow-cooking pot. Cover and cook on low for 4 to 6 hours (depending on size and shape). Cool, peel and place in large bowl. Mash until smooth. Add butter, ¼ cup brown sugar, lemon peel, juice and salt; mix well. Spoon into greased 1½-qt. baking dish. Sprinkle remaining ⅓ cup brown sugar and almonds on top. Bake in 350°F. oven for 40 to 50 minutes. Makes 6 to 8 servings. This recipe not suitable for Cornwall or Sears tray-type Crockery Cookers.

CANDIED YAMS & CRANBERRIES

6 medium yams or sweet
  potatoes
½ cup butter or
  margarine
¾ cup light brown sugar
  (lightly packed)

2 cups fresh cranberries
1 tsp. salt
⅛ tsp. pepper

Wash yams or potatoes; drain but do not dry. Set in
slow-cooking pot. Cover and cook on low for 4 to 6
hours (depending on size and shape). Peel and cut
into quarters. Place in 2-quart casserole. In medium
saucepan, melt butter; add sugar, cranberries, salt and
pepper. Cook, stirring constantly, over medium heat
until cranberries pop and sugar dissolves. Pour over
yams in casserole.° Cover and bake in 350°F. oven for
30 minutes. Makes 6 servings. This recipe not suitable
for Cornwall or Sears tray-type Crockery Cookers.

° Casserole may be refrigerated and baked later. If
cold, add 10 to 15 minutes to oven time.

SAUSAGE-STUFFED YAMS

6 medium yams or sweet
  potatoes
2 tbs. butter or
  margarine, melted
2 tbs. milk

1 egg
1 tsp. salt
¼ tsp. dried oregano
  leaves
4 ozs. smoky link sausage

Wash yams; drain but do not dry. Set in slow-cooking
pot. Cover and cook on low for 4 to 6 hours (depending on size and shape). Cut tops from yams; carefully
scoop out centers and mash in large bowl. Add butter,
milk, egg, salt, and oregano; beat until smooth. Add
sausage; mix well. Pile into yam shells. Bake in 400°F.
oven for 15 to 20 minutes. Makes 6 servings. This
recipe is not suitable for Cornwall or Sears tray-type
Crockery Cookers.

CREOLE ZUCCHINI

2 lbs. zucchini
1 small green pepper, chopped
1 small onion, chopped
1 clove garlic, minced
1 tsp. salt
¼ tsp. pepper
4 tomatoes, peeled and chopped
2 tbs. butter or margarine
2 tbs. minced parsley

Cut zucchini into ¼-inch slices. In slow-cooking pot, combine zucchini with green pepper, onion, garlic, salt, and pepper. Top with chopped tomatoes, then butter. Cover and cook on high for about 2 hours or until tender. Sprinkle with chopped parsley. Makes 6 to 7 servings. This recipe is not suitable for Cornwall or Sears tray-type Crockery Cookers.

STUFFED HONEYED SWEET POTATOES

5 to 6 sweet potatoes
½ cup soft butter
¼ cup light cream
2 tbs. honey
2 tbs. dark rum
½ tsp. cardamom
¼ tsp. salt
2 tbs. chopped walnuts

Wash potatoes; drain excess water. Place damp potatoes in slow-cooking pot. Cover and cook on low 5 to 6 hours or until done.* Cut off the top third of each potato lengthwise and scoop out, leaving a ¼-inch shell. Mash potato pulp with butter, cream, honey, rum, cardamom, and salt. Return mixture to shell. Top with walnuts. Arrange on shallow baking sheet. Bake in 425°F. oven for 15 minutes. Makes 5 to 6 servings. This recipe is not suitable for Cornwall or Sears tray-type Crockery Cookers.

* If desired, potatoes may be refrigerated at this point, then scooped out and filled just before serving. Add about 5 or 10 minutes to baking time if potatoes are cold.

SLOW COOKERY SWEET POTATOES

5 medium sweet potatoes or yams

Wash potatoes. Drain but do not dry. Set in slow-cooking pot. Cover and cook on low for 4 to 6 hours (depending on size and shape of potatoes). Split tops and serve hot with butter. For a sweet potato casserole, let potatoes cool; then peel and slice. This recipe is not suitable for Cornwall or Sears tray-type Crockery Cookers.

ZUCCHINI CASSEROLE

1 lb. lean ground beef	¼ tsp. basil
1 medium onion, chopped	½ tsp. salt
3 (8-oz.) cans tomato	⅛ tsp. seasoned pepper
sauce	4 to 5 zucchini
½ cup dry red wine	¼ cup grated Parmesan
¼ tsp. oregano	cheese
⅛ tsp. garlic salt	

In large skillet or slow-cooking pot with browning unit, cook beef and onion until meat loses its red color. Pour off excess fat. In slow-cooking pot, combine beef and onion with tomato sauce, wine, oregano, garlic salt, basil, salt, and pepper. Cover and cook on low for 4 to 5 hours.° Pour into greased shallow baking dish. In the meantime, cook whole zucchini in a regular pan of boiling salted water about 15 minutes or until barely tender. Cut lengthwise in halves and arrange, cut side up, on top of meat mixture in baking dish. Sprinkle with cheese. Bake in 350°F. oven 30 to 45 minutes. Makes 5 to 6 servings.

° May be refrigerated at this point and assembled the next day if desired. Bake an additional 5 to 10 minutes if you refrigerate it.

MIXED VEGETABLES EN POT

2 (10-oz.) packages frozen
mixed vegetables,
partially thawed
½ cup finely chopped
celery
2 (10¾-oz.) cans
condensed cream of
celery soup
½ tsp. seasoned salt
1 packet (about ½ oz.)
toasted onion dip mix
½ cup water
2 tbs. melted butter or
margarine

In slow-cooking pot, combine mixed vegetables with celery. In medium bowl, mix soup with seasoned salt, dry dip mix, water, and melted butter. Pour over vegetables in pot. Cover and cook on low for 4 to 5 hours or until vegetables are tender. Makes 6 servings.

STEWED TOMATOES

4 or 5 large ripe tomatoes
2 tbs. butter or margarine
1 medium onion, thinly
sliced
½ cup chopped celery
¼ cup chopped green
pepper
½ tsp. sugar
½ tsp. dried sweet basil
1 small bay leaf
1 tsp. salt
⅛ tsp. pepper
2 tbs. chopped parsley

Quickly dip tomatoes in boiling water; remove skin. Quarter tomatoes; remove core and seeds. In slow-cooking pot, combine all ingredients except parsley. Cover and cook on low for 8 to 9 hours. Remove bay leaf. Sprinkle top with parsley. Makes 4 to 5 servings.

APPETIZERS & BEVERAGES

You will have more time with your guests when you serve hot beverages or appetizers in a slow cooker.

Several hours before a party, combine the ingredients for one of the hot drinks. Turn the control on the slow cooker to **LOW** and the drink will be ready to serve when your guests arrive. What's more, it will be kept hot in a slow cooker without fear of scorching, boiling over or sticking to the pan. Each person can serve himself whenever he is ready for a cup of cheer. This is an especially good way to plan a get-together after the theater or ball game. You can plug in the slow cooker with ingredients for a hot drink, leave for the show, and return with your friends and immediately offer them a hot drink. Exact times are relatively unimportant when brewing most hot punches. After several hours, the various fruit juices blend together for a smooth taste. However, if left on too many hours over the suggested time, they may become slightly bitter.

Hot appetizers stay hot in a slow cooker. There is no reason for you to rush back and forth to the range to serve hot snacks. Just heat them in a slow cooker. Guests can help themselves whenever they are ready for another hot snack.

If you heat cheese or bean dip in a slow cooker, it will be the right consistency and temperature for all to enjoy. You take it easy by letting your pot keep your favorite appetizer hot at your next party. Relax! *Enjoy* the festivities.

ZIPPY TOMATO APPETIZER

1 (10½-oz.) can
condensed beef broth
½ tsp. dried marjoram,
crushed

1 (46-oz.) can vegetable
juice cocktail
1 tbs. lemon juice

In slow-cooking pot, combine broth, marjoram, vegetable juice cocktail, and lemon juice. Cover and heat on low for 2 to 3 hours. Serve hot from slow-cooking pot. Makes 8 to 10 servings.

HOME-STYLE TOMATO JUICE

10 to 12 large tomatoes
1 tsp. salt
1 tsp. seasoned salt

¼ tsp. pepper
1 tbs. sugar

Wash and drain tomatoes. Remove core and blossom ends. Place in slow-cooking pot. Cover and cook on low 4 to 6 hours or until tomatoes are done. Press through sieve or food mill. Add seasonings; chill. Makes about 4 cups juice.

SPICY TOMATO JUICE COCKTAIL

4 lbs. fresh tomatoes
    (12 to 14)
½ cup chopped celery
¼ cup chopped onion
2 tbs. lemon juice
1½ tsp. sugar
1 tsp. salt

1 tsp. prepared
    horseradish
1 tsp. Worcestershire
    sauce
⅛ tsp. bottled hot pepper
    sauce

Wash tomatoes; remove stem ends and cores. Chop tomatoes. In slow-cooking pot, combine tomatoes, celery, and onions. Cover and cook on low for 8 to 10 hours. Press through food mill or sieve. Return juice to pot. Cook on high for 30 minutes. Add lemon juice, sugar, salt, horseradish, Worcestershire sauce, and hot sauce. Cook on high for another 10 minutes. Chill. Makes about 6 cups.

APPETIZER RIBS

3 to 4 lbs. spareribs. cut
    into individual ribs*
Salt and pepper
2 cups water
Garlic salt

1 (8-oz.) bottle Russian
    salad dressing
1 (6-oz.) can pineapple
    juice

Sprinkle ribs with salt and pepper. Place in slow-cooking pot; pour water over them. Cover and cook on low for 6 to 7 hours or until tender. Drain. Arrange ribs on broiler pan; sprinkle with garlic salt. Make sauce by combining salad dressing and pineapple juice. Brush ribs with half the sauce. Broil until brown; turn, brush other side and brown. Makes 8 to 10 appetizer servings.

* If possible, ask the butcher to cut each rib in half, crosswise, so they will be a more convenient size to handle as an appetizer.

FINGER DRUMSTICKS

1½ pounds chicken wings (12 to 15)	½ tsp. salt
Salt and pepper	¼ tsp. ground ginger
1 cup chicken bouillon	⅛ tsp. pepper
1 tbs. cornstarch	3 tbs. lemon juice
¼ cup sugar	2 tbs. soy sauce
	⅛ tsp. garlic salt

Cut off and discard wing tips; divide each wing in half by cutting through joint with a sharp knife. Sprinkle wings with salt and pepper. Place in slow-cooking pot. Pour bouillon over chicken. Cover and cook on low for 4 to 5 hours or until tender. Drain; place on broiler pan. Meanwhile, in small saucepan, combine cornstarch with sugar, salt, ginger, pepper, lemon juice, soy sauce and garlic salt. Simmer, stirring constantly, until mixture thickens. Brush some sauce on chicken; brown under broiler. Turn; brush sauce on chicken and brown other side. Makes about 25 to 30 appetizers. Recipe may be doubled for a party. Keep appetizers hot and serve from slow-cooking pot.

CURRIED ALMONDS

2 tbs. melted butter	½ tsp. seasoned salt
1 tbs. curry powder	1 lb. blanched almonds

Combine butter with curry and seasoned salt. Pour over almonds in slow-cooking pot and mix to coat well. Cover and cook on low for 2 to 3 hours. Turn to high. Uncover pot and cook for 1 to 1½ hours. Serve hot or cold, as a snack.

CHILI NUTS

¼ cup soft or melted
butter
2 (12-oz.) cans cocktail
peanuts

1 (1⅝-oz.) package chili
seasoning mix

In slow-cooking pot, pour butter over nuts; sprinkle in dry chili mix. Toss together. Cover pot and heat on low for 2 to 2½ hours. Turn control to high. Remove top and cook on high for 10 or 15 minutes. Serve warm or cool in small nut dishes. Makes about 5 cups.

ALL-AMERICAN SNACK

3 cups thin-pretzel sticks
4 cups Wheat Chex
4 cups Cheerios
1 (13-oz.) can salted
peanuts
1 tsp. garlic salt

1 tsp. celery salt
½ tsp. seasoned salt
2 tbs. grated Parmesan
cheese
¼ cup melted butter

In large mixing bowl or slow-cooking pot, mix together pretzels, cereals, and peanuts. Sprinkle with garlic salt, celery salt, seasoned salt, and cheese. Pour melted butter over all; toss until well mixed. Cover and cook in slow-cooking pot on low 3 to 4 hours. Uncover the last 30 to 40 minutes. Serve as appetizer or snack. Makes about 3 quarts.

EAST INDIAN SNACK

1 (5-oz.) can crisp
Chinese noodles
1 (6¼-oz.) package salted
cashew nuts
2 cups Rice Chex

½ cup toasted coconut
1 tsp. curry powder
¼ tsp. ground ginger
¼ cup melted butter
1 tbs. soy sauce

In mixing bowl or slow-cooking pot, mix together noodles, cashews, Rice Chex, and coconut. Sprinkle with curry and ginger. Add butter and soy sauce. Toss until well mixed. Cover and cook in slow-cooking pot on low 3 to 4 hours. Uncover the last 30 to 40 minutes. Serve as appetizer or snack. Makes about 6 cups.

LIVER PÂTÉ BON APPETIT

1 lb. chicken livers
½ cup dry wine
1 tsp. instant chicken
bouillon or 1 bouillon
cube
1 tsp. minced parsley
1 tbs. instant
minced onion

¼ tsp. ginger
½ tsp. seasoned salt
1 tbs. soy sauce
¼ tsp. dry mustard
¼ cup soft butter
1 tbs. brandy

Combine chicken livers in slow-cooking pot with wine, bouillon, parsley, onion, ginger, seasoned salt, soy sauce, and mustard. Cover and cook on low 4 to 5 hours. Let stand in liquid until cool. Drain and place in blender or food grinder. Add butter and brandy. Blend or mix until smooth. Serve with crackers or toast. Makes about 1½ cups.

SHORT-CUT FONDUE DIP

2 (10¾-oz.) cans
  condensed cheese soup
2 cups (½ lb.) grated
  sharp cheddar cheese
1 tbs. Worcestershire
  sauce
1 tsp. lemon juice

1 (.01-oz.) packet
  freeze-dried chopped
  chives
Celery sticks
Cauliflower, cut into
  flowerets (uncooked)
Corn chips (optional)

Combine condensed soup, grated cheese, Worcestershire sauce, lemon juice, and chives. Cover and heat on low in slow-cooking pot for 2 to 2½ hours. Stir until smooth and well blended. Keep hot in the pot. Dip celery sticks, cauliflower, and corn chips into cheese mixture. Makes 8 to 10 servings.

REFRIED BEAN DIP

1 (20-oz.) can refried
  beans
1 cup shredded cheddar
  cheese
½ cup chopped green
  onions

¼ tsp. salt
2 tbs. bottled taco
  sauce
Tortilla chips

In slow-cooking pot, combine beans with cheese, onions, salt, and taco sauce. Cover and cook on low for 2 to 2½ hours. Serve hot from the pot. Dip tortilla chips into mixture.

CHILI CON QUESO

1 lb. pasteurized process cheese spread
1 (1-lb.) can chili without beans
4 green onions, chopped
1 (4-oz.) can chopped green chili peppers

Mix all ingredients in slow-cooking pot. Cover and cook on low 2 to 3 hours. Serve hot from the pot. Use as dip for corn chips. Makes about 4 cups.

HOT SPICED CLARET

2 tbs. sugar
2 tbs. lemon juice
½ tsp. ground cinnamon
¼ tsp. ground nutmeg
½ cup hot water
1 (4/5-qt.) bottle claret wine

In slow-cooking pot, combine sugar, lemon juice, cinnamon, nutmeg, and water. Stir until well blended. Pour in wine. Cover pot; heat on low 2 to 2½ hours. Serve hot from the pot. Makes 6 to 8 servings.

WINTER WARM-UP

1 (4/5-qt.) bottle sherry or muscatel
6 cups orange juice
1 tsp. ground cardamom

In slow-cooking pot, combine wine with orange juice and cardamom. Cover and heat on low for 2 to 3 hours. Ladle into heat-proof glasses or mugs. Makes 10 to 12 servings.

TROPICAL TEA WARMER

6 cups boiling water
6 tea bags
⅓ cup sugar
2 tbs. honey

1½ cups orange juice
1½ cups pineapple juice
1 orange, sliced
(unpeeled)

Pour boiling water over tea bags in slow-cooking pot.*
Cover and let stand 5 minutes. Remove tea bags. Stir
in sugar, honey, orange juice, pineapple juice, and
orange slices. Cover and heat on low for 2 to 3 hours;
serve from pot. Makes 10 servings.

* If slow-cooking pot is cold, warm first with hot tap
water.

MEDITERRANEAN COFFEE

2 qts. strong hot coffee
¼ cup chocolate syrup
⅓ cup sugar
4 cinnamon sticks
1½ tsp. whole cloves
½ tsp. anise flavoring

Peel of 1 orange, in strips
for twists
Peel of 1 lemon, in strips
for twists
Whipped cream

Combine coffee, chocolate syrup, sugar, cinnamon
sticks, cloves, and anise in slow-cooking pot. Cover
and cook on low for 2 to 3 hours. Serve in cups with
twist of lemon, twist of orange, and cap of whipped
cream in each. Makes 12 servings.

HOT BUTTERED PUNCH

¾ cup brown sugar
4 cups water
¼ tsp. salt
¼ tsp. nutmeg
½ tsp. cinnamon
½ tsp. allspice

¾ tsp. ground cloves
2 (1-lb.) cans jellied
  cranberry sauce
1 qt. pineapple juice
Cinnamon sticks
Butter

In slow-cooking pot, combine brown sugar with water, salt, nutmeg, cinnamon, allspice, and cloves. Break up cranberry sauce with fork. Add cranberry sauce and pineapple juice to pot. Cover and heat on low for 3 to 4 hours. Serve hot in individual mugs with cinnamon sticks. Dot each mug with butter. Makes about 3 quarts.

MULLED CIDER

2 qts. apple cider
¼ cup packed brown
  sugar
2 sticks cinnamon

1 tsp. whole cloves
⅛ tsp. ground ginger
1 orange, sliced
  (unpeeled)

Combine ingredients in slow-cooking pot. Cover and heat on low for 2 to 5 hours or longer. Serve from pot. Makes 10 to 12 servings.

PADRÉ PUNCH

1 (6-oz.) can frozen
orange juice, partially
thawed
3 orange juice cans
water
1 qt. apple cider

5 whole cloves
2 cinnamon sticks
1 tsp. ground nutmeg
¾ tsp. ground ginger
Orange slices

In slow-cooking pot, combine orange juice with water, cider, cloves, cinnamon, nutmeg and ginger. Cover and heat on low for 4 to 6 hours (or longer). Garnish with orange slices. Keep hot and serve punch in slow-cooking pot. Makes 7 to 10 servings. Recipe may be doubled if your slow-cooking pot is large enough.

BISHOP'S WINE

2 tbs. whole cloves
3 whole unpeeled
oranges
2 (⅘-qt.) bottles dry red
wine

½ cup sugar
1 stick cinnamon

Stick whole cloves into peel of whole oranges. Prick skin several times with fork. Drop into bottom of slow-cooking pot. Pour in wine, sugar, and cinnamon. Cover and cook on low for 3 to 4 hours. Serve hot from the pot. If desired, cut oranges into wedges as garnish for each serving. Makes 10 servings.

APPLE BRANDY BREW

1 (4/5-qt.) bottle apple-
    flavored wine
2 cups apple cider

1 cup peach brandy
1 cinnamon stick

Combine ingredients in slow-cooking pot. Cover and heat on low for 3 to 4 hours. Serve hot. Makes 8 servings.

HOT WINE CRANBERRY PUNCH

1 pt. cranberry juice
    cocktail
1 cup water
¾ cup sugar
2 sticks cinnamon

6 whole cloves
1 (4/5-qt.) bottle
    Burgundy wine
1 lemon, thinly sliced
    (unpeeled)

Combine ingredients in slow-cooking pot. Heat on low for 1 to 2 hours. Strain and serve hot. May be kept hot and served from slow-cooking pot set on lowest setting. Makes 6 to 8 mugs or 10 to 12 punch-cup servings.

SPICED APRICOT PUNCH

1 (46-oz.) can apricot
    nectar
3 cups orange juice
½ cup brown sugar,
    packed

2 tbs. lemon juice
3 sticks cinnamon
½ tsp. whole cloves

In slow-cooking pot, combine apricot nectar, orange juice, brown sugar, and lemon juice. Tie cinnamon and cloves in small cheesecloth bag; add to juices. Cover and heat on low for 2 to 5 hours. Serve hot from pot. Makes 12 servings.

HOT SPICY LEMONADE PUNCH

4 cups cranberry juice
⅔ cup sugar
1 (12-oz.) can lemonade
  concentrate, thawed
4 cups water

2 tbs. honey
6 whole cloves
2 cinnamon sticks, broken
1 lemon, sliced
  (unpeeled)

In slow-cooking pot, combine cranberry juice, sugar, lemonade concentrate, water and honey. Tie cloves and cinnamon in small cheesecloth square. Add spice bag and lemon slices to juices. Cover and cook on low for 3 to 4 hours. Remove spice bag. Keep hot in slow-cooking pot. Makes 9 to 10 cups.

HOT MINT MALT

6 chocolate-covered,
  cream-filled mint
  patties
5 cups milk

½ cup chocolate
  malted milk powder
1 tsp. vanilla
Whipped cream

In slow-cooking pot, combine mint patties with milk, malted milk powder, and vanilla. Heat on low for 2 hours. Beat with rotary beater until frothy. Pour into cups; top with whipped cream. Makes 6 servings.

SOUPS & SANDWICHES

After you have made a few soups, you will be convinced that slow cookers were made just for this purpose. They bring out the flavors by retaining all of the natural meat and vegetable juices.

If you are tired of rushing home after work or shopping to make dinner, plan to have a hearty main dish soup. Start with leftover turkey, chicken or ham bone. Then you can build almost any traditional soup with a few seasonings and vegetables. Put the ingredients into your slow cooker before you leave. When you get home, it will be ready to serve in large portions directly from the pot. To complete the meal, heat thick slices of buttered French bread. What could be easier?

Some soups are glamorous enough to serve your guests. *Green Vegetable Chowder* with sour cream added at the last minute is one example. *Bouillabaise* is quite a conversation piece in itself.

Notice how the cooking times vary for these soups. At such low temperatures most soups don't care if they are cooked longer. At the minimum recommended cooking time, lift the lid and stick a fork into the meat and several of the larger vegetable pieces to see whether they are done. Try not to keep the lid off any longer than necessary because steam and heat escape very fast. It takes a long time to replace the heat loss after you've replaced the lid.

Try some of the short-cut soups which start with a packaged mix or canned product as a base. They are surprisingly good and they take less cooking time than soups "made from scratch."

Slow cookers work fine as serving pots for hot sandwiches. *Sloppy Joes, Sloppy Janes* and *Chili Dogs* will be the favorites of the younger generation. You can combine the sandwich mixture in your slow cooker and leave it for several hours. Teenagers can serve themselves and make their own sandwiches or the Cub Scouts will devour it after their meeting.

Ham Stuffed Rolls and *Over-Stuffed Tuna Egg Sandwiches* can be completely assembled and kept warm in your pot. Don't plan to keep these sandwiches much longer than the suggested time because the bread will become soggy.

DUMPLING SOUP

1 lb. beef stew meat,
cut into 1-inch cubes
1 (1⅜ oz.) pkg. onion
soup mix
6 cups water, hot
2 carrots, peeled
and shredded
1 stalk celery, finely
chopped

1 tomato, peeled and
chopped
1 cup packaged biscuit
mix
1 tbs. finely chopped
parsley
6 tbs. milk

In slow-cooking pot, sprinkle beef with dry onion soup
mix. Pour hot water over meat. Stir in carrots, celery
and tomato. Cover and cook on low for 4 to 6 hours
or until meat is tender. Turn control on high. In small
bowl, combine biscuit mix with parsley. Stir in milk
with fork until mixture is moistened. Drop dumpling
mixture into slow-cooking pot with a teaspoon. Cover
and cook on high for 30 minutes. Makes 5 to 6 servings.

SHORT-CUT ITALIAN VEGETABLE SOUP

1 envelope country
vegetable-with-noodles
soup mix
2 cups boiling water
1 onion, chopped
2 carrots, peeled and
chopped
1 (8-oz.) can tomato
sauce

1 tsp. salt
⅛ tsp. pepper
1 (16-oz.) can kidney
beans, drained
1 (16-oz.) can whole
kernel corn, with
liquid
Grated Parmesan cheese

Warm slow-cooking pot with hot tap water. In pot,
stir dry soup mix into very hot water. Add onions, carrots, tomato sauce, salt and pepper. Cover and cook
on low for 4 to 6 hours. Turn control to high; add beans
and corn. Cover and cook on high for about 30 minutes. Sprinkle with cheese. Makes 4 to 6 servings.

HEARTY ALPHABET SOUP

½ lb. beef stew meat or
  round steak
1 (1-lb.) can stewed
  tomatoes
1 (8-oz.) can tomato
  sauce
1 cup water

1 package onion soup mix
1 (10-oz.) package frozen
  mixed vegetables,
  partially thawed
½ cup uncooked
  alphabet noodles

Cut beef into small cubes. In slow-cooking pot, combine meat with stewed tomatoes, tomato sauce, water, and soup mix. Cover and cook on low for 6 to 8 hours. Turn to high; add vegetables that have been partially thawed, and noodles. Cover and cook on high 30 minutes or until vegetables are done. Makes 5 to 6 servings.

GEORGIA PEANUT SOUP

3 cups chicken broth or
  bouillon
¼ cup finely chopped
  celery
¼ tsp. salt
1 small onion, finely
  chopped
2 tbs. butter or
  margarine

½ cup peanut butter
1 cup milk or light cream
¼ cup flour
¼ cup water
¼ cup finely chopped
  peanuts (optional)

Combine chicken stock, celery, salt, onion, butter, and peanut butter in slow-cooking pot. Cover and cook on high for 2 to 3 hours. Add milk and flour that has been dissolved in ¼ cup water. Cook on high 15 minutes or until slightly thickened, stirring several times. Sprinkle peanuts over each serving, if desired. Makes 4 servings.

TURKEY NOODLE SOUP*

1 turkey carcass, broken
  into several pieces
2 qts. water
1 tsp. salt
¼ tsp. pepper
1 onion, chopped
2 stalks celery, chopped
1 carrot, chopped

1 tbs. dried parsley
  leaves
½ tsp. marjoram leaves
1 bay leaf
3-inch square
  cheesecloth
6 ozs. noodles, cooked
  and drained

Combine turkey carcass and water in slow-cooking
pot. Add salt, pepper, onion, celery, and carrot. Place
parsley, marjoram and bay leaf in center of cheesecloth. Gather up sides and tie. Drop in pot with turkey.
Cover and cook on low for 5 to 6 hours. Remove carcass and spice bag from pot. Take meat off bones; return meat to broth. Drop cooked noodles into pot with
meat. Cover and cook on high for 20 to 30 minutes.
Makes 8 servings.

* This recipe is designed for a 4½ quart slow-cooking
pot. For 3½ quart or smaller slow-cooking pots, use
chunks of turkey meat cut off the bones, or chicken
parts.

SWEDISH CABBAGE SOUP*

2 lamb shanks
2 beef bouillon cubes
½ tsp. pepper
1 tsp. salt
1 tbs. whole allspice
1 cup chopped leeks
½ cup peeled, diced
  parsnips
1 cup peeled, diced
  carrots

½ cup thinly sliced
  celery
2 medium potatoes,
  peeled and diced
¼ cup minced parsley
2 qts. water
2 qts. shredded cabbage

Place lamb shanks in slow-cooking pot with bouillon cubes, pepper, and salt. Tie allspice in cheesecloth. Add allspice, leeks, parsnips, carrots, celery, potatoes, parsley, and water to pot. Cover and cook on low for 7 to 9 hours or until meat is tender. Remove allspice and meat from pot. Cut meat off bones; dice and return to pot. Skim off fat from top of soup. Turn control to high. Add cabbage. Cover and cook on high for 25 to 30 minutes or until cabbage is done. Makes 8 servings.

* This recipe designed for 4½ quart or larger slow-cooking pot.

MINESTRONE SOUP

1 lb. beef shank or
  stew meat
6 cups water
1 onion, chopped
1 tsp. salt
1 tsp. powdered thyme
2 tbs. minced parsley
¼ tsp. pepper
1 (16-oz.) can tomatoes,
  cut up

1 zucchini, thinly sliced
1 (16-oz.) can garbanzo
  beans, drained
2 cups chopped cabbage
1 cup small elbow
  marcaroni, uncooked
¼ cup grated Parmesan
  cheese

In slow-cooking pot, combine beef with water, onion, salt, thyme, parsley, pepper, and tomatoes. Cover and cook on low for 7 to 9 hours. Remove beef bones; cut up meat and return to pot. Turn control to high. Add zucchini, beans, cabbage, and macaroni. Cover and cook on high for 30 to 45 minutes or until vegetables are tender. Sprinkle with cheese. Makes 8 to 10 servings.

OLD-FASHIONED VEGETABLE SOUP

2 lbs. soup bones or
  1 lb. beef short ribs
2 qts. water
1 tsp. salt
1 tsp. celery salt
1 small onion, chopped
1 cup diced carrots
½ cup diced celery

2 cups diced potatoes
1 (1-lb.) can whole kernel
  corn, not drained
1 (1-lb.) can tomatoes,
  cut up
2 turnips, peeled and
  finely chopped

Place meat, water, salt, celery salt, onion, carrots, and celery in slow-cooking pot. Cover and cook on low 4 to 6 hours. Remove bones; chop meat and return to pot. Add potatoes, corn, tomatoes, and turnips. Cover and cook on high for 2 to 3 hours. Makes 8 to 10 servings.

Minestrone Soup
Courtesy Thermador

DOWN EAST CORN CHOWDER

3 cups fresh corn, cut
from cob or 2 (16-oz.)
cans whole kernel corn,
drained
2 medium potatoes,
peeled and finely
chopped
1 onion, finely chopped
1 tsp. salt

½ tsp. seasoned salt
⅛ tsp. pepper
2 cups chicken broth or
bouillon
2 cups milk
¼ cup butter or
margarine
Ground mace

Combine corn, potatoes, onion, salt, seasoned salt, pepper, and broth in slow-cooking pot. Cover and cook on low 7 to 9 hours. Pour into blender and puree until almost smooth. Chill overnight, if desired, or return to pot. Stir in milk and butter. Cover and cook on high for 1 hour. Pour into bowls; sprinkle with mace. Makes 6 to 8 servings.

FRENCH ONION SOUP

3 large onions, thinly
sliced
½ cup butter or
margarine
2 tbs. instant beef
bouillon or 6 bouillon
cubes
4 cups hot water

1 tsp. Worcestershire
sauce
½ tsp. salt
4 slices toasted French
bread
¼ cup grated Parmesan
cheese

In large skillet or slow-cooking pot with browning unit, cook onions in butter until lightly browned. In pot, combine browned onions in butter with bouillon, water, Worcestershire sauce, and salt. Cover and cook on low 4 to 6 hours. Top each bowl with toasted French bread sprinkled with cheese. Makes 4 servings. Recipe may be doubled, kept hot in slow-cooking pot, and served from pot.

CREAM OF CAULIFLOWER SOUP

1 medium head
  cauliflower, cut into
  flowerets
1 stalk celery, cut into
  1-inch pieces
1 medium onion,
  chopped
1 tsp. salt

⅛ tsp. white pepper
1 qt. chicken or turkey
  broth
1 cup light cream
½ tsp. Worcestershire
  sauce
Nutmeg

Combine cauliflower, celery, onion, salt, pepper, and broth in slow-cooking pot. Cover and cook on low 6 to 8 hours. Force mixture through sieve or puree in blender. Return to pot. Add cream and Worcestershire sauce. Cook on high 5 to 10 minutes to heat. Sprinkle with nutmeg. Makes 6 servings.

GREEN VEGETABLE CHOWDER

6 to 8 medium leeks
2 small potatoes, peeled
  and diced
3 cups chicken broth or
  bouillon
1 (10-oz.) package frozen
  peas, thawed

½ cup coarsely chopped
  watercress leaves
2 tbs. butter
1 tsp. salt
½ tsp. seasoned salt
⅛ tsp. pepper
½ cup dairy sour cream

Trim and clean leeks; slice crosswise. In slow-cooking pot, combine leeks with potatoes, broth, peas, watercress, butter, salts, and pepper. Cover and cook on low 5 to 7 hours or until vegetables are tender. Pour ⅓ of mixture at a time into blender and whirl until smooth. Return mixture to pot. Turn control to high. Stir in sour cream; cook on high for 15 to 20 minutes or until hot. Spoon into bowls; garnish with a few watercress leaves. Makes 4 to 6 servings.

HERBED SPINACH SOUP

3 green onions, finely
  chopped
3 sprigs parsley
¼ small head lettuce,
  sliced
1 bunch fresh spinach
2 tbs. butter or margarine
½ tsp. salt

⅛ tsp. pepper
1 tsp. tarragon
4 (10½-oz.) cans beef
  consommé
½ cup light cream
1 hard-cooked egg,
  chopped

In slow-cooking pot, combine onions, parsley, lettuce, spinach, butter, salt, pepper, tarragon, and consommé, Cover and cook on low 4 to 6 hours. Pour into blender (part of the mixture at a time). Blend until vegetables are finely chopped. Turn slow-cooking pot on high. Pour blended mixture into pot. Stir in cream. Cook on high 20 to 30 minutes. Serve hot, with garnish of chopped hard-cooked egg. Makes 8 servings.

TAVERN SOUP

¼ cup finely chopped
  celery
¼ cup finely chopped
  carrot
¼ cup finely chopped
  green pepper
¼ cup finely chopped
  onion
3 (13¾-oz.) cans chicken
  broth

2 tbs. butter or margarine
1 tsp. salt
¼ tsp. pepper
⅓ cup flour
3 cups (¾ lb.) grated
  sharp cheddar cheese
1 (12-oz.) can light beer
  (at room temperature)

Combine celery, carrot, green pepper, and onion in slow-cooking pot. Add broth, butter, salt, and pepper. Cover and cook on low for 5 to 6 hours. Strain mixture; puree vegetables in blender and return to pot with broth. Turn control to high. Dissolve flour in small amount of water; add to broth. Add cheese, ½ cup at a time, stirring until blended. Pour in beer. Cover and cook on high 15 to 20 minutes. Makes 6 to 8 servings.

LENTIL SOUP—CRESCENTI STYLE*

1 to 2 lbs. beef neck bones
   or beef shanks
3 carrots, peeled and
   chopped
3 medium potatoes,
   peeled and chopped
1 large onion, peeled
   and chopped
3 stalks celery with tops,
   chopped
3 tomatoes, chopped

⅛ tsp. marjoram
5 cups water
5 beef bouillon cubes,
   crumbled
½ lb. lentils
1 tsp. salt
¼ tsp. pepper
2 zucchini, chopped
½ head cabbage,
   shredded

In slow-cooking pot, combine beef with carrots, potatoes, onion, celery, tomatoes, marjoram, water, bouillon cubes, lentils, salt, and pepper. Cover and cook on low for 9 to 10 hours or until lentils are tender. Remove beef bones from pot; cut off meat and return to pot. Turn control to high. Add zucchini and cabbage. Cover pot and cook on high for 30 to 45 minutes or until vegetables are tender. Makes 8 servings. This is a thick, hearty soup, similar to a stew.

*This recipe designed for 4½ quart or larger slow-cooking pot. Cut recipe in half for smaller pot.

SPLIT PEA SOUP

1 (1-lb.) package split
   peas
1 ham bone (with some
   meat left on) or
   2 ham hocks
1 carrot, diced

1 onion, diced
1 stalk celery, diced
2 qts. water
1 tsp. salt
¼ tsp. pepper

Combine ingredients in slow-cooking pot. Cover and cook on low for 8 to 10 hours. Remove ham bone; cut meat off, dice, and return meat to soup. Makes 8 servings.

BEEF SHANK SOUP

1 to 1½ lbs. beef shanks
8 cups water
1 onion, chopped
½ cup chopped celery
1 carrot, chopped
1½ tsp. salt
2 tbs. finely chopped
  parsley

1 bay leaf
4 whole peppercorns
1 clove garlic, cut in half
¼ tsp. dried thyme
  leaves
Cheesecloth (about
  4-inch square)

In slow-cooking pot, combine beef with water, onion, celery, carrot, salt and parsley. Place bay leaf, peppercorns, thyme and garlic in center of cheesecloth. Pull up on each corner, forming a bag and tie. Drop in pot with meat. Cover and cook on low 6 to 8 hours, or until meat is tender. Remove spice bag. Ladle soup into bowls. Makes 6 to 8 servings.

This is a basic beef soup. For variations, before the last hour of cooking, add any one of the following: Two 1-lb. cans drained kidney beans and one sliced green pepper; or 3 cups cooked mixed vegetables; or 1 cup narrow uncooked noodles. Cover and cook for one hour.

NEW ENGLAND CLAM CHOWDER

¼ lb. salt pork or bacon,
  cut in small cubes
1 onion, chopped
2 medium potatoes,
  peeled and diced
½ tsp. salt
⅛ tsp. pepper

3 cups water
2 (7-oz.) cans minced
  clams or 1 pint fresh-
  shucked clams, cut up
2 cups light cream or
  evaporated milk
Paprika

Saute pork with onion in a skillet or in slow-cooking pot with browning unit. Combine sauteed pork, onion, potatoes, salt, pepper, and water in pot. Cover and cook on low 5 to 7 hours. Turn control to high. Add clams and cream. Cover and cook on high for 15 minutes. Sprinkle with paprika. Makes 6 to 7 servings.

BOUILLABAISE

1 carrot, chopped
1 onion, chopped
1 clove garlic, minced
1 (1-lb.) can tomatoes,
  cut up
3 cups water
2 bay leaves
2 cups beef bouillon
¼ cup chopped parsley
½ tsp. dried thyme
  leaves, crushed

1 tbs. salt
1 tsp. lemon juice
1/16 tsp. powdered
  saffron
1 lb. large uncooked
  shrimp, shelled
1 lb. fresh or frozen fish
  fillets, thawed and cut
  into 2-inch chunks
2 uncooked lobster tails,
  cut into 2-inch chunks*

In large slow-cooking pot, combine carrot, onion, garlic, tomatoes, water, bay leaves, bouillon, parsley, thyme, salt, lemon juice, and saffron. Cover and cook on low for 6 to 8 hours. Strain; return broth to pot. Turn control to high. Add shrimp, fish fillets, and lobster.* Cover pot and cook on high for 20 to 30 minutes or until seafood is done. Serve in large bowls with French bread. Makes 6 to 7 servings.

*If lobster tails are cooked, add them about 5 minutes before serving.

OVERSTUFFED TUNA-EGG SALAD ROLLS

1 (9¼-oz.) can tuna,
  drained
3 hard-cooked eggs,
  chopped
½ cup finely chopped
  celery
1 tbs. chopped chives

2 tbs. sweet pickle relish
½ cup mayonnaise
¼ tsp. salt
⅛ tsp. pepper
6 to 7 hamburger buns
Foil

In mixing bowl, combine drained tuna, eggs, celery, chives, relish, mayonnaise, salt, and pepper. Spoon mixture into split hamburger buns. Wrap each bun in foil. Place in slow-cooking pot. Cover and heat on low for 2 to 2½ hours. Serve hot from the pot. Makes 6 to 7 servings.

HOT CHICKEN SALAD

2 cups diced cooked chicken (or turkey)
1½ cups diced celery
1 cup ham-flavored croutons
½ cup slivered toasted almonds
1½ tsp. grated Parmesan cheese

4 tbs. mayonnaise
1 tbs. lemon juice
½ tsp. salt
¼ tsp. curry powder (optional)
1 cup crushed potato chips
½ cup grated cheddar cheese

In slow-cooking pot, combine chicken, celery, croutons, almonds and Parmesan cheese. Toss together to mix. In small bowl, combine mayonnaise, lemon juice, salt and curry powder. Stir until well blended. Pour over chicken mixture. Stir to coat thoroughly. Cover and cook on low 2 to 3 hours. Sprinkle with potato chips and cheddar cheese. Turn to high and cook another 20 minutes or until cheese melts.

CHILI DOGS

1 (15-oz.) can chili with beans
1 (6-oz.) can tomato paste
¼ cup minced green pepper

¼ cup minced onion
1 tsp. prepared mustard
½ tsp. salt
½ tsp. chili powder
8 to 10 frankfurters
8 to 10 frankfurter buns

In slow-cooking pot, combine chili with beans, tomato paste, green pepper, onion, mustard, salt, and chili powder. Cover and cook on low for 3 to 4 hours. In large saucepan, drop frankfurters into boiling water; simmer several minutes. Toast buns. Serve a frankfurter on each bun. Spoon chili mixture onto frankfurters. Makes 8 to 10 servings.

Recipe may be doubled for a larger group. Keep chili mixture hot in slow-cooking pot. Serve from the pot.

SLOPPY JANE SANDWICHES

1 package (about 10) frankfurters, sliced
1 (28-oz.) can baked beans
1 tsp. prepared mustard
1 tsp. instant minced onion
⅓ cup chili sauce*
5 to 6 frankfurter buns, toasted

In slow-cooking pot, combine frankfurters with beans, mustard, onion, and chili sauce. Cover and cook on low for 2 to 3 hours. Spoon over toasted frankfurter buns. Makes 5 to 6 servings.

*Bottled tomato sauce similar to catsup.

BARBECUE BEEF SANDWICHES

2 cups thinly sliced cooked beef or pork
2 tbs. instant minced onion
1 tbs. brown sugar
2 tsp. paprika
1 tsp. crushed oregano
1 tsp. chili powder
1 tsp. cracked pepper
½ tsp. salt
1 bay leaf
1 clove garlic, minced
1 cup catsup
¼ cup water
1 tbs. salad oil
¼ cup tarragon vinegar
2 tbs. Worcestershire sauce
2 or 3 drops liquid smoke

Combine ingredients in slow-cooking pot. Cover and cook on low 4 to 6 hours. Remove and discard bay leaf. Serve hot over French rolls or buttered toast. Makes 4 to 5 servings.

SLOPPY JOES

1½ lbs. lean ground beef
1 small onion, minced
2 stalks celery, minced
1 (12-oz.) bottle chili
  sauce*
2 tbs. brown sugar

1 tbs. Worcestershire
  sauce
1 tsp. salt
2 tbs. sweet pickle relish
⅛ tsp. pepper

In large skillet or slow-cooking pot with browning unit, cook beef with onion and celery until meat loses its red color. Pour off excess fat. In slow-cooking pot, combine meat, onion, and celery with remaining ingredients. Cover and cook on low for 3 to 4 hours. Spoon over toasted hamburger buns or French rolls. Makes 4 to 6 servings. Recipe may be doubled and mixture kept warm in slow-cooking pot for after-the-game party.

*Bottled tomato sauce similar to catsup.

REUBEN SANDWICHES

1 (1-lb) can sauerkraut
Sliced corned beef
  brisket (not canned)*
¼ lb. Swiss cheese,
  sliced

Sliced rye bread
Sandwich spread or
  Thousand Island
  dressing

Drain sauerkraut in sieve; then on paper towels until very dry. Place sauerkraut in bottom of slow-cooking pot. Arrange layer of corned beef slices on sauerkraut. Top with cheese slices. Cover and cook on low 3 to 4 hours. Toast slices of bread; spread generously with sandwich spread. Spoon ingredients from slow-cooking pot onto toasted bread, maintaining layers of sauerkraut, meat and cheese. Serve open-faced or closed. Makes three to four sandwiches.

*See recipe for Corned Beef.

HAM-STUFFED FRENCH ROLLS

2 cups finely chopped
  cooked ham
2 hard-cooked eggs,
  finely chopped
2 tbs. minced green
  onion
2 tbs. chopped ripe olives
  (optional)

1 tsp. prepared mustard
1 tsp. sweet pickle relish
½ cup small cubes
  cheddar cheese
⅓ cup mayonnaise
6 large or 8 small French
  rolls

Combine ham with eggs, onion, olives, mustard, relish, cheese, and mayonnaise. Cut off tops *or* one end of rolls; scoop out most of soft center. Fill with ham mixture. Replace top or end of roll. Place filled rolls in slow-cooking pot. Cover and heat on low for 2 to 3 hours. Rolls may be kept hot and served from the pot. Makes 6 to 8 servings.

WELSH RAREBIT

1 (12-oz.) can beer
1 tbs. dry mustard
1 tsp. Worcestershire
  sauce
½ tsp. salt

⅛ tsp. pepper
1 lb. processed American
  cheese, cut into cubes
1 lb. sharp cheddar
  cheese, cut into cubes

In slow-cooking pot, combine beer, mustard, Worcestershire sauce, salt and pepper. Cover and cook on high for 1 to 2 hours or until mixture boils. Add cheese a little at a time, stirring constantly, until all cheese has melted. Heat on high for 20 to 30 minutes with lid off, stirring frequently. Serve hot over toast or toasted English muffins. Garnish with strips of crisp bacon and tomato slices. Makes 4 to 6 servings.

MAIN DISHES

Every family has a few favorite meal-in-one dishes. Just add a salad and you have a complete meal. Slow-cooking pots are perfect for such meals because you can combine most of the ingredients and let them cook while you are busy on another project.

I have included a few classics and popular combination dishes which lend themselves admirably to slow cooking. Several of these feature fish or seafood. Because most fish or seafood should be cooked quickly, it is not suitable for slow cooking. For this reason, you should use your pot for sauce-making. Put vegetables and seasonings in your slow cooker and add the seafood at the end of the cooking time. *Paella in a Pot* is a good example of this. It is quite an exotic dish to make—and you can serve it directly from the pot. But—the fish and rice are added at the very last part of the cooking session.

Rice is not at its best when cooked longer than recommended on the package. Cook it first, then add to the pot a short time before serving.

The same principle applies to most pasta—macaroni and spaghetti products. They provide real added taste pleasure without straining the budget. When fixing pasta, remember that sauce flavors are enhanced by long times in the slow cooker, but the pasta should be added near the end of the cooking time.

Another point to remember is to add cheese, milk, cream and sour cream shortly before serving. Dairy products are at their best when refrigerated as long as possible, then added for flavor, texture and nutrition near the end of the cooking period or served with the food.

If you want a creamy sauce for a main dish, cook the vegetables, spices and meats in water, bouillon or tomato sauce for a special flavor. Then add the cream or milk and thicken later.

Follow all of these main dish suggestions and you will be able to experiment on your own. Don't forget the versatility of packaged seasoning mixes which blend well with many Italian and Mexican-type dishes. You will discover countless variations and combinations you can tailor-make for your family.

JAMBALAYA

1 broiler-fryer chicken,
  cut up
3 onions, chopped
1 carrot, sliced
1 clove garlic, minced
½ tsp. oregano
½ tsp. basil
1 tsp. salt
⅛ tsp. pepper
1 (14-oz.) can tomatoes,
  cut-up
1 lb. shelled, raw shrimp
2 cups cooked rice

In slow-cooking pot, combine chicken with onions, carrots, garlic, oregano, basil, salt, pepper and tomatoes.
Cover and cook on low 4 to 5 hours. Turn control to
high. Add shrimp and rice. Cover and cook on high
for 30 to 40 minutes or until shrimp is done. Makes
5 to 6 servings.

SHRIMP MARINARA

1 (16-oz.) can peeled
  tomatoes, cut up
2 tbs. minced parsley
1 clove garlic, minced
½ tsp. dried basil
1 tsp. salt
¼ tsp. pepper
1 tsp. dried oregano
1 (6-oz.) can tomato paste
½ tsp. seasoned salt
1 lb. cooked shelled
  shrimp
Grated Parmesan cheese
Cooked spaghetti

In slow-cooking pot, combine tomatoes with parsley,
garlic, basil, salt, pepper, oregano, tomato paste, and
seasoned salt. Cover and cook on low 6 to 7 hours.
Turn control to high. Stir in shrimp; cover and cook
on high for 10 to 15 minutes. Serve, topped with
Parmesan cheese, over cooked spaghetti. Makes 4
servings.

1/Here's how to shell shrimp. Hold tail firmly in one hand. With other hand separate legs with thumb and peel back the shell. Snap off the tail.

2/Distribute chicken and vegetables in slow-cooking pot.

PAELLA IN A POT

1 (2½ to 3-lb.) frying
  chicken, cut up
2 carrots, cut into sticks
2 onions, cut into eighths
1 (13¾-oz.) can chicken
  broth
1 clove garlic, minced

2 tbs. chopped pimiento
½ tsp. salt
¼ tsp. ground oregano
1/16 tsp. saffron powder
2 cups cooked rice
½ lb. shelled raw shrimp
12 small clams in shells

In slow-cooking pot, combine chicken with carrots,
onions, broth, garlic, pimiento, salt, oregano, and
saffron. Cover and cook on low for 4 to 6 hours. Turn
control to high. Add cooked rice, shrimp, and clams.
Cover and cook on high for another 30 to 50 minutes
or until shrimp is done. Makes 6 to 8 servings.

SHELL CASSEROLE

1 lb. lean ground beef
1 small onion, chopped
1 tsp. salt
¼ tsp. garlic powder
1 tsp. Worcestershire
  sauce
¼ cup flour
1¼ cups hot water

2 tsp. beef bouillon
2 tbs. red wine
6 ozs. large shell-shaped
  macaroni
1 (2-oz.) can sliced
  mushrooms, drained
1 cup dairy sour cream

In skillet or slow-cooking pot with browning unit, cook
ground beef and onion until red color disappears.
Drain meat; place in slow-cooking pot. Stir in salt,
garlic powder, Worcestershire sauce and flour. Add
water, bouillon and wine; mix well. Cover and cook
on low for 2 to 3 hours. In meantime, cook macaroni
according to package directions. Add cooked macaroni, mushrooms and sour cream to slow-cooking pot;
stir to mix ingredients. Cover and cook on high for 10
to 15 minutes. Makes 4 to 5 servings.

TORTILLA PIE

1½ lbs. lean ground beef
1 package enchilada
  sauce mix
2 (8-oz.) cans tomato
  sauce
½ tsp. salt
1 cup water
1 large onion, finely
  chopped

1 (2¼-oz.) can sliced, ripe
  olives
Heavy-duty foil (about
  15 inches long)
8 to 10 corn tortillas
1 cup grated cheddar
  cheese

Sauce:

1 (8-oz.) can tomato sauce
½ cup water

1 package spicy cheese
  dip mix (about ½ oz.)

In skillet or slow-cooking pot with browning unit, cook beef until crumbly; drain off excess fat. In mixing bowl, combine dry enchilada sauce mix with tomato sauce, salt, and water; stir in onion, olives, and browned beef. Line slow-cooking pot with foil by making a "nest" in the bottom. Spoon 2 tbs. meat-sauce mixture on foil in bottom. Arrange alternate layers of tortillas and meat sauce, ending with a layer of sauce on top. Cover and cook on low for 4 to 6 hours. Sprinkle with cheese. Cook another 5 minutes. Picking up sides of foil liner, lift tortilla pie out of pot. Slide onto serving dish. Cut into wedges; serve with sauce. Makes 6 servings.

Sauce: In small saucepan, combine tomato sauce, water, and dry cheese dip mix. Cover and simmer for 5 minutes. Serve hot.

MOCK CHILI RELLENO

2 tsp. butter
1 (4-oz.) can whole green
  chilies
½ lb. grated cheddar
  cheese
½ lb. grated Monterey
  Jack cheese

1 (14½-oz.) can tomato
  slices, drained
4 eggs
¾ cup evaporated milk
2 tbs. flour

Grease sides and bottom of slow-cooking pot with
butter. Remove seeds from chilies; cut into strips.
Place half the chilies in bottom of pot. Layer with
cheddar cheese, then rest of chilies, Jack cheese, and
tomatoes. Separate eggs. Beat whites until stiff. Fold
in slightly beaten yolks and milk. Add flour. Pour over
top of tomatoes. Cover and cook on high for 2 to 3
hours. Serve while piping hot. Makes 4 to 5 servings.

MOIST CORNBREAD

3 eggs
2 cups milk
2 tbs. melted butter

1 (15-oz.) pkg. cornbread
  mix

Beat eggs in medium bowl; beat in milk, butter and
cornbread mix. Pour into greased 8-cup baking dish
or spring-form pan. Place in slow-cooking pot and
cover with several paper towels. Cover and cook on
high for 2 to 3 hours.

VEGETARIAN SPAGHETTI

1 package spaghetti sauce
  mix
1 (8-oz.) can tomato sauce
1 cup water
4 zucchini
1 small eggplant
1 small green pepper, cut
  into 1-inch cubes

3 medium tomatoes, cut
  into small wedges
½ tsp. salt
½ lb. uncooked spaghetti
¼ lb. mozzarella cheese,
  grated

In slow-cooking pot, mix dry spaghetti sauce mix with
tomato sauce and water. Cut zucchini into ½-inch
crosswise slices. Peel eggplant; slice thinly, then cut
each slice into quarters. Add zucchini, eggplant, green
pepper, tomatoes, and salt to spaghetti sauce. Cover
and cook on low for 4 to 6 hours or until vegetables
are tender. In meantime, cook spaghetti according to
package directions; drain well. When ready to serve,
top each serving of spaghetti with vegetable-sauce
mixture. Sprinkle with cheese. May be served as main
dish or as accompaniment to thinly sliced roast beef.
Makes 6 servings.

CALIFORNIA TAMALE PIE

1 lb. lean ground beef
¾ cup yellow corn meal
1½ cups milk
1 egg, beaten
1 package chili seasoning
mix
1 tsp. seasoned salt
1 (1-lb.) can tomatoes,
cut up

1 (1-lb.) can whole kernel
corn, drained
1 (2¼-oz.) can sliced ripe
olives, drained
1 cup grated cheddar
cheese

In skillet or slow-cooking pot with browning unit, cook meat until crumbly; drain. In large bowl, mix corn meal, milk, and egg. Add drained meat, dry chili seasoning mix, seasoned salt, tomatoes, corn, and olives. Pour into slow-cooking pot. Cover and cook on high for 3 to 4 hours. Sprinkle cheese over top. Cook another 5 minutes. Makes 6 to 8 servings.

CHEESE FONDUE

1 lb. natural Swiss cheese,
shredded
6 oz. natural or process
Gruyere cheese,
shredded
2 tsp. cornstarch

1 clove garlic, halved
1⅓ cups sauterne wine
1 tbs. lemon juice
French bread, cut into
bite-size chunks

Combine Swiss and Gruyere cheese with cornstarch. Rub inside of slow-cooking pot with cut garlic; then discard garlic. Pour sauterne and lemon juice into pot; turn control on high. Heat for 20 to 30 minutes or until very hot. Gradually add cheese (a handful at a time) stirring constantly until melted. After cheese is completely melted, turn control to low to keep warm. Dip chunks of French bread into hot fondue. If fondue gets too thick, turn to high, add one or two extra tablespoons of warmed sauterne and stir until blended. Makes 8 to 10 servings.

DAD'S HAM & POTATOES

4 or 5 baking potatoes
¼ cup butter or
  margarine
¼ cup flour
½ tsp. salt
2 cups milk or light cream

½ tsp. Worcestershire
  sauce
2 cups cooked ham, cut
  into chunks
½ cup grated cheddar
  cheese

Wash potatoes; drain but do not dry. Place in slow-cooking pot. Cover and cook on low for 6 to 8 hours. Cool slightly.* Peel and slice. In saucepan, melt butter. Add flour and salt; stir until blended. Slowly add milk, stirring constantly. Cook several minutes, stirring until smooth and thickened. Stir in Worcestershire sauce, then potatoes and ham. Spoon into 1½-qt. baking dish. Sprinkle with cheese. Heat in 350°F. oven for 30 to 40 minutes. Makes 4 to 5 servings. This recipe not suitable for Cornwall or Sears tray-type Crockery Cookers.

*At this point, potatoes may be refrigerated and the recipe continued the next day, if desired.

BEANS

Because slow cookers are up-to-date electric cousins of the old-fashioned bean pot, bean dishes cook fine in them. Modern-day homemakers like to prepare beans in slow cookers because they can spend the day away from home while long, slow cooking is mingling compatible flavors to create the old-fashioned taste of Grandmother's bean pot.

Directions for cooking dried beans suggest the long-soaking method. If it is inconvenient for you to soak beans overnight, you can add six cups of water to one pound of beans. Bring to a boil and simmer two minutes. Remove from heat, cover and let stand one hour. Then follow the directions for cooking each bean recipe. If you live at a high altitude, boil the beans first, then let them soak overnight in the same water before cooking.

Most bean recipes may be cooked longer than the times indicated or they may be cooked one day and re-heated in the slow cooker for use the next day.

If you like your beans saucy, don't pour off any of the liquid in which the beans were soaked—leave as much juice in the pot as possible during the long cooking process.

Most of the bean recipes serve 6 to 8 people. If you have a 4½ quart or larger slow cooker, you can double any of these recipes for a party. While you are getting everything else ready, the beans cook with no fuss or bother. Then they stay hot until serving time in a slow cooker. In case you hadn't guessed—slow cookers are ideal buffet servers.

CONGRESSIONAL BEAN SOUP

1 lb. dried small white
  beans
8 cups water
1 meaty ham bone or 2
  cups diced cooked ham
1 cup finely chopped
  celery

1 onion, finely chopped
2 tbs. finely chopped
  parsley
1 tsp. salt
¼ tsp. pepper
1 bay leaf

In large pan, heat beans in water. Boil gently for 2 minutes; turn off heat and let stand 1 hour.* Pour into slow-cooking pot. Add remaining ingredients. Cover and cook on low for 12 to 14 hours or until beans are very soft. Remove bay leaf and ham bone. Cut meat off bone; return meat to beans. Serve hot. Makes 6 to 8 servings.

*May be soaked overnight if preferred.

PORTUGUESE BEAN SOUP

1 cup dried red beans
6 cups water
2 onions, sliced
1 clove garlic, minced
¼ lb. salt pork, cut into
  thick slices
3 potatoes, peeled and
  diced

¼ tsp. allspice
1 (8-oz.) can tomato paste
1 tsp. salt
3 tsp. beef bouillon, or
  3 bouillon cubes

In slow-cooking pot, soak beans in water overnight. Cover and cook on high for 2 to 3 hours or until tender. Add remaining ingredients. Cover and cook on low for 6 to 8 hours. Makes 6 to 8 servings.

BAKED BEAN SOUP

1 (1-lb. 12-oz.) can baked
  beans
6 slices cooked bacon,
  chopped
2 tbs. bacon drippings
2 tbs. finely chopped
  onion

1 (1-lb.) can stewed
  tomatoes
1 tbs. brown sugar
1 tbs. vinegar
1 tsp. seasoned salt

Combine all ingredients in slow-cooking pot. Cover
and cook on low for 4 to 6 hours. Makes 5 to 6 servings.

BOSTON BAKED BEANS

1 lb. dried small white
  beans
6 cups water
1 tsp. salt
½ cup molasses

2 tsp. dry mustard
¼ cup brown sugar
1 medium onion,
  chopped
¼ lb. salt pork

Pour beans into slow-cooking pot; add water. Soak
overnight or at least 6 hours. Cover pot and cook on
high for 2 to 3 hours or until beans are tender. Drain,
saving liquid. Mix 1 cup of the liquid with salt, molasses, mustard, brown sugar and onion. Cut salt pork
into 2 or 3 pieces. In slow-cooking pot, combine
drained beans with molasses mixture and pork. Cover
and cook on low for 10 to 12 hours. Keep hot in slow-
cooking pot, using it as serving dish. Makes 6 to 8
servings.

VERMONT BAKED BEANS WITH HAM

1 lb. dried baby lima
  beans
6 cups water
2 cups diced baked ham
  or 2 ham hocks
1 tbs. prepared mustard

½ cup brown sugar
½ cup maple-flavored
  syrup
1 tsp. salt
¼ tsp. pepper

Soak beans in water overnight in slow-cooking pot.
Cover and cook on high for 2 to 3 hours or until tender
but not mushy. Drain, saving liquid. Return beans to
slow-cooking pot. Stir in ham, mustard, brown sugar,
maple syrup, salt, pepper, and ½ cup liquid from
beans. Cover and cook on low for 8 to 10 hours. If
using ham hocks, cut ham off bones. Return meat to
beans. Makes 6 servings.

BAKED BEAN CASSOULET

1 lb. dried red or kidney
  beans
6 cups water
1 medium onion, chopped
¼ cup molasses
1 (15-oz.) can tomato
  sauce
1 tsp. salt

¼ tsp. dry mustard
⅛ tsp. pepper
1 tbs. Worcestershire
  sauce
1 (12-oz.) pkg. smoked
  sausage links, cut into
  1-inch slices

In slow-cooking pot, soak beans in water overnight.
Cover and cook on high for 2 to 3 hours or until
tender. Drain, saving liquid. Combine 1 cup of the
liquid with onion, molasses, tomato sauce, salt, mustard, pepper and Worcestershire sauce. Mix with
drained beans in slow-cooking pot. Cover and cook
on low for 10 to 12 hours. Add sausage the last hour
of cooking. Makes 6 to 8 servings.

SOUR CREAM LIMAS

1 lb. dried baby lima
  beans
6 cups water
¼ cup melted butter
½ cup brown sugar

¼ cup molasses
2 tbs. prepared mustard
1 tsp. salt
1 cup dairy sour cream

Soak beans in water overnight. Cook in slow-cooking pot on high for 2 to 3 hours, or until tender. Drain thoroughly; pour beans into large mixing bowl. Combine butter, brown sugar, molasses, mustard and salt. Mix with drained beans. Stir in sour cream. Spoon into baking dish. Heat in 350°F. oven for 30 to 40 minutes or until bubbly. Makes 6 to 8 servings.

PIZZA BEANS

1 lb. pinto beans
6 cups water
4 medium tomatoes,
  peeled and diced
1 onion, chopped
¼ cup chopped green
  pepper
1 clove garlic, crushed

2 tsp. salt
½ tsp. oregano leaves,
  crushed
¼ tsp. rosemary, crushed
1 cup shredded
  mozzarella cheese
¼ cup grated Romano or
  Parmesan cheese

Soak beans in water overnight. In slow-cooking pot, cook soaked beans in water on high for 2 to 3 hours, or until tender but not mushy. Drain, saving liquid. In slow-cooking pot, combine beans with tomatoes, onion, green pepper, garlic, salt, oregano, and rosemary. Add 2 cups liquid from beans. Cover and cook on low for 8 to 10 hours. Turn control to high; add mozzarella and Romano cheeses. Cook, uncovered, on high for 15 to 20 minutes. Turn heat off; let stand a few minutes before serving to let beans absorb some of the juice. Makes 6 to 8 servings.

SOUTHWESTERN HAM & BEANS

1 lb. dried pinto beans	4 small dried chilies
Water	2 medium ham hocks

In slow-cooking pot, cover pinto beans with water. Soak for about 12 hours. Drain water; re-cover with water. Add chilies. Cover and cook on low for 10 to 12 hours. Add ham hocks; cover and cook on low another 10 to 12 hours. Remove rind and bone from ham hocks; cut meat into small pieces and return to pot with beans. Mix well. Makes 6 to 8 servings.

RANCH STYLE BEANS

1 lb. lean ground beef	1 (16-oz.) can kidney
1 envelope green onion	beans, drained
dip mix	1 cup catsup
2 (16-oz.) cans pork and	2 tbs. prepared mustard
beans in tomato sauce	2 tsp. vinegar

In large skillet or slow-cooking pot with browning unit, cook meat until red color disappears. Drain off excess fat. In slow-cooking pot, combine beef, dry dip mix, undrained pork and beans, drained kidney beans, catsup, mustard, and vinegar. Cover and cook on low for 3 to 4 hours. Makes 8 servings.

ZIPPY BEANS AND HOMINY

2 slices bacon, cooked
and drained
1 (7-oz.) can green chili
salsa
2 tsp. prepared mustard
1 tsp. Worcestershire
sauce

1 (1-lb.) can kidney beans,
drained
1 (1-lb.) can yellow
hominy, drained

Combine ingredients in slow-cooking pot. Cover and
cook on low for 4 to 5 hours. Serve. Especially good
with barbecued hamburgers. Makes 6 servings.

SWEET-SOUR BEAN TRIO

4 slices bacon
1 onion, chopped
¼ cup brown sugar
1 tsp. prepared mustard
1 clove garlic, crushed
1 tsp. salt
¼ cup vinegar

1 (1-lb.) can lima beans,
drained
1 (1-lb.) can baked beans,
drained
1 (1-lb.) can kidney beans,
drained

Cook bacon in skillet or slow-cooking pot with browning unit. Crumble bacon. Combine cooked bacon and
2 tbs. bacon drippings with onion, brown sugar, mustard, garlic, salt and vinegar. Mix with three kinds of
beans in slow-cooking pot. Cover and cook on low
for 6 to 8 hours. Makes 6 to 8 servings.

SAVORY TOMATO LIMAS

2 cups (1 lb.) large dry
  lima beans
6 cups water
1 onion, chopped
1 clove garlic, minced
1 tbs. prepared mustard
1 tbs. Worcestershire
  sauce

1 tsp. salt
½ tsp. chili powder
1 (10½-oz.) can
  condensed tomato soup
2 tbs. vinegar
2 tbs. brown sugar
¼ lb. salt pork, cut into
  several pieces

Soak beans in water overnight. Pour into slow-cooking
pot. Cover and cook on high for 2 hours. Drain. Combine onion, garlic, mustard, Worcestershire sauce,
salt, chili powder, tomato soup, vinegar, and sugar.
Mix with beans in slow-cooking pot. Top with pork.
Cover and cook on low for 9 to 11 hours. Makes 8
servings.

MAC'S KIDNEY BEANS

4 slices bacon, chopped
3 (15-oz.) cans kidney
  beans, drained
1 cup chili sauce*

½ cup sliced green
  onions
⅓ cup brown sugar

In small skillet, cook bacon, saving 2 tbs. drippings.
In slow-cooking pot, add bacon and 2 tbs. bacon drippings to drained kidney beans, chili sauce and green
onions. Sprinkle top with brown sugar. Cover pot and
cook on low for 4 to 6 hours. Keep beans hot and serve
from pot. Makes 8 to 10 servings.

*Bottled tomato sauce similar to catsup.

BLACK-EYED PEAS, MEXICAN STYLE

1 lb. dried black-eyed
  peas
6 cups water
¼ lb. salt pork, cut into
  thick slices

1 clove garlic, minced
1 tsp. salt
¼ tsp. pepper
¼ tsp. dried oregano

In slow-cooking pot combine black-eyed peas with water. Soak overnight. Cook soaked beans in water on high for 2 to 2½ hours or until tender, but not mushy. Turn control on low. Stir in salt pork, garlic, salt, pepper and oregano. Cover and cook on low 8 to 10 hours. Drain and serve.

BREADS & CAKES

If you think it takes a genius to bake breads or cakes in a slow cooker, give some of these recipes a try so you can tell your friends how easy it is.

There are a few tricks to remember when "baking" in one of these pots. First, turn the control to **HIGH** (or to the setting which is equivalent to the **HIGH** used in my recipes). The **LOW** setting is too low to give breads and cakes tne texture you expect. With breads, remember to cover the container with a lid or foil. Tie the lid or foil onto the container and place the container on a metal rack or trivet inside the pot. If you don't have a metal rack or trivet to fit your slow cooker, crumple foil and place it in the bottom of the pot to support the baking container. Pour 2 cups of hot water around the container to provide steam for cooking the bread.

When using a deep-fryer type slow cooker, check frequently to make sure the water hasn't evaporated. Add more water if needed.

As a rule, it is not a good idea to remove the lid or foil from the bread container during the first 2 hours of cooking. After that, check the bread by inserting a toothpick in the mixture. If the toothpick comes out clean, the bread is done.

When using a standard cake mix, as in the recipe for *Banana Nut Cake* or *Applesauce Spice Cake*, the procedure is slightly different. Cakes are "baked" in a pan set directly on the bottom of the slow cooker, similar to the way you would do it in an oven. It is not necessary to use a trivet or water. Instead of covering the uncooked cake mixture with foil or a lid, cover the top with four or five layers of paper towels. Because there is more moisture in a slow cooker than in an oven it is necessary to compensate for this with the paper towels to help absorb the moist top of the cake mix. Also, leave the lid of your slow cooker slightly open to let extra moisture escape.

Try the *Plum Pudding!* It is cooked in a mold inside your slow cooker. This recipe calls for a metal rack or trivet for the mold and warm water around it. The water helps to steam the pudding, giving a moist texture to all its yummy spices and fruits.

The type and kind of container to use for breads and cakes will depend on the size of your pot. In addition to molds and coffee cans, spring forms or small bundt pans make excellent containers. The following containers hold approximately the same amount of batter so you can substitute one for another:

1 (2-lb.) coffee can   6- or 7-cup mold
2 (1-lb.) coffee cans   1½-quart baking dish
3 (16-oz.) vegetable cans

Many different containers work well for baking. Here two soufflé dishes do the trick.

Spring form pans work well, as do coffee cans and cake molds.

Oster Super Pot is large enough to hold a tube pan.

Cover pan or mold with foil for steam baking.

Tie foil tightly to keep bread dry when steam baking.

Place trivet or meat rack in bottom of pot to keep pan out of water for steam baking.

Place pan or mold on rack.
Pour about 2 cups of
water in bottom of pot.
Water should be just below
baking container.
Cover and cook on **HIGH**.

To bake a regular cake
mix, place pan directly on
bottom of pot.
Put 4 to 5 paper towels on
top of pan to absorb extra
moisture. Cover and
cook on **HIGH**.
For this dry baking
method, no
water is used around pan.

POUND CAKE

1 (16-oz.) pkg. pound
  cake mix

⅔ cup water
2 eggs

Blend cake mix with water and eggs in mixing bowl
on low speed until moistened. Beat on medium speed
for 3 minutes, scraping the bowl frequently. Pour into
a greased and floured 8-cup mold or spring form pan.
Place in slow-cooking pot. Cover mold with 4 or 5
paper towels. Cover pot and cook on high 2½ to 3½
hours. When cake is done, top will be slightly moist
and a toothpick inserted in the center comes out clean.
Cool on rack 5 minutes before removing cake from
pan. Turn out of pan and cool. Serve plain, frosted or
with fruit. Makes 6 servings.

BOSTON BROWN BREAD

1 cup corn meal
1 cup rye flour
1½ tsp. baking soda
1 tsp. salt
1 cup whole wheat flour

¾ cup molasses
2 cups sour milk or
  buttermilk
1 cup raisins

In large bowl, combine corn meal, rye flour, soda, and salt; add wheat flour. In small bowl, stir molasses into sour milk; add to dry ingredients, a little at a time. Stir just enough to blend. Add raisins. Spoon into two greased (1-lb.) coffee cans. Cover with foil; tie. Place cans on metal rack in bottom of slow-cooking pot. Pour 2 cups hot water around cans. Cover pot and cook on high for 2½ to 3 hours. Remove cans from pot. Let stand 5 to 10 minutes. Turn bread out on cooling rack. Serve warm with butter.

GINGER BROWN BREAD

1 (14-oz.) pkg. ginger-
  bread mix
¼ cup yellow corn meal

1 tsp. salt
1½ cups milk
½ cup raisins

Combine gingerbread mix with corn meal and salt in large bowl; stir in milk until mixture is evenly moist. Beat at medium speed with electric mixer for 2 minutes. Stir in raisins. Pour into greased and floured 6- or 7-cup mold. Cover with foil; tie. Put trivet or metal rack in slow-cooking pot. Pour 2 cups hot water in pot. Place filled mold on rack or trivet. Cover pot and cook on high for 3 to 4 hours or until bread is done. Remove from pot; cool on rack 5 minutes. Loosen edges with knife; turn out on rack and cool slightly. Serve warm with butter or cream cheese.

SLOW-COOKING POTS	2 (1-lb.) Coffee Cans	1 (2-lb.) Coffee Can	3 (15-oz.) or (16-oz.) Vegetable Cans	4-cup Mold	7-cup Mold*	9-cup Mold*	8-inch Spring-Form Pan
Cornwall 4-Quart **				X	X		
Cornwall 4 1/2-Quart			X	X	X	X	
Cornwall 8-Quart	X		X	X	X	X	X
Dominion Crock-A-Dial			X	X	X		
Farberware 5-Quart		X		X	X	X	X
Grandinetti 3 1/2-Quart			X	X	X		
Grandinetti 5-Quart	X		X	X	X	X	X
Hamilton Beach Crock-Watcher			X	X	X		
Hamilton Beach Simmer-on			X	X	X		

	1	2	3	4	5	6	7
Nesco Pot Luck Cooker		X	X	X	X	X	
Oster 8-Quart Super Pot	X	X	X	X	X	X	X
Penneys Slow Cooker/Fryer		X	X	X	X	X	X
Presto 5-Quart	X	X	X	X	X	X	
Regal Pot O' Plenty		X	X	X	X	X	X
Rival 3 1/2-Quart Crock-Pot		X	X	X	X	X	
Rival 4 1/2-Quart Crock-Pot	X	X	X	X	X	X	X
Sears 4-Quart**		X	X	X	X		
Sears 5-Quart		X	X	X		X	
Sunbeam Crocker-Cooker-Fryer		X	X	X	X	X	X
West Bend 6-Quart	X	X	X	X	X	X	X

*7- and 9-cup molds are not always shaped the same.

**Integrated model (crockery pot and heating unit combined)

STEAMED MOLASSES BREAD

2 cups all-bran cereal
2 cups whole wheat flour
2 tsp. baking powder
1 tsp. salt
1 tsp. baking soda

1 cup raisins
1 egg
1¾ cups sour milk or
    buttermilk
½ cup dark molasses

In medium bowl, combine bran, flour, baking powder, salt, baking soda, and raisins. In another bowl, beat the egg; add sour milk and molasses. Blend in dry ingredients; do not overbeat. Pour into greased and floured 8-cup mold or can. Cover with foil; tie. Place rack in slow-cooking pot. Pour 2 cups hot water in pot. Place covered bread container on rack. Cover pot and cook on high for 3 to 4 hours. Turn bread out on cooling rack. Serve warm or cool.

PEANUT BUTTER LOAF

¾ cup hot water
¾ cup peanut butter
¾ cup milk
½ tsp. sugar
¼ tsp. salt

1 egg
2 cups flour
4 tsp. baking powder
¾ cup chopped salted
    peanuts

In large bowl, pour hot water over peanut butter. Stir in milk, sugar, salt, egg, flour, and baking powder. Mix well. Add peanuts. Grease 5- or 6-cup mold. Spoon bread mixture into mold. Cover with foil and tie. Place mold on rack in slow-cooking pot. Pour 2 cups hot water around mold. Cover pot and cook on high for 2 to 3 hours or until done. Remove from pot. Let bread stand in mold for 10 minutes; turn out on cooling rack. Serve warm or cool; spread with butter, marmalade, or jam.

CRANBERRY NUT BREAD

2 cups (½ lb.) fresh
cranberries
1 medium cooking apple,
peeled, cored, and cut
into chunks
½ cup walnuts
2 cups flour
1 cup sugar

1½ tsp. baking powder
½ tsp. baking soda
½ tsp. salt
6 tbs. soft butter
1 egg
1 tbs. grated orange peel
½ cup orange juice

Put cranberries, apple, and walnuts through coarsest
blade of food grinder; set aside. Combine flour, sugar,
baking powder, baking soda, and salt in a deep bowl.
Cut in butter until size of peas. Stir in egg, orange
peel, and juice; then the cranberry-apple mixture. Stir
until blended. Spoon into greased 2-qt. mold or two
1-lb coffee cans. Cover with foil and tie. Place filled
mold or coffee cans on metal rack in slow-cooking pot.
Pour 2 cups hot water around mold. Cover pot and
cook on high for 2½ to 3 hours. Remove mold from
pot. Let stand several minutes; turn bread out on
cooling rack. Serve warm with butter. Especially good
as a coffee cake for brunch; with fresh fruit plate, or
chicken salad for lunch.

BANANA NUT BREAD

⅓ cup shortening
½ cup sugar
2 eggs
1¾ cups all-purpose flour
1 tsp. baking powder

½ tsp. baking soda
½ tsp. salt
1 cup mashed ripe bananas
½ cup chopped walnuts

Cream together shortening and sugar; add eggs and beat well. Sift dry ingredients; add to creamed mixture alternately with banana, blending well after each addition. Stir in nuts. Pour into well-greased 4- to 6-cup mold. Cover with foil and tie. Pour 2 cups hot water in slow-cooking pot. Place mold on rack or trivet in pot. Cover and cook on high 2 to 3 hours or until bread is done. Serve warm or cool, with butter, peanut butter or cream cheese.

DATE AND NUT LOAF

1½ cups boiling water
1½ cups chopped dates
1¼ cups sugar
1 egg
2 tsp. baking soda

½ tsp. salt
1 tsp. vanilla
1 tbs. melted butter
2½ cups flour
1 cup walnuts, chopped

In large bowl, pour boiling water over dates. Let stand 5 to 10 minutes. Stir in sugar, egg, baking soda, salt, vanilla, and butter. In small bowl, mix flour with nuts; stir into date mixture. Pour into two greased 1-lb. coffee cans or one 8-cup mold. Cover with foil and tie. Place cans or mold on rack in slow-cooking pot. Pour 2 cups hot water around cans. Cover pot and cook on high for 2½ to 3 hours or until done. Remove from pot. Let bread stand in coffee cans 10 minutes; turn out onto cooling rack. Slice and spread with butter, cream cheese, or peanut butter.

PUMPKIN NUT BREAD

1½ cups flour
1¼ tsp. soda
1 tsp. salt
1 tsp. ground cinnamon
½ tsp. ground nutmeg
1 cup canned pumpkin

1 cup sugar
½ cup buttermilk
1 egg
2 tbs. soft butter
1 cup chopped pecans

Sift flour, soda, salt, and spices. Combine pumpkin, sugar, buttermilk, and egg in mixing bowl. Add dry ingredients and butter; beat until well blended. Stir in nuts. Spread in well-greased and floured 4- to 5-cup mold or 1-lb. coffee can. Cover with foil. Place rack in slow-cooking pot. Pour 2 cups hot water in pot. Place covered bread container on rack. Cover pot and cook on high 3 to 4 hours. Turn out on cooling rack. Serve warm or cool.

PLUM PUDDING

4 slices bread, torn up
1 cup milk
2 slightly beaten eggs
1 cup light brown sugar
¼ cup orange juice
6 oz. finely chopped suet
(or ask butcher to grind it)
1 tsp. vanilla
1 cup flour
1 tsp. soda

½ tsp. salt
2 tsp. ground cinnamon
1 tsp. ground cloves
1 tsp. ground mace
2 cups raisins
1 cup pitted dates, cut up
½ cup chopped, mixed candied fruits and peels
½ cup coarsely chopped walnuts

Soak bread in milk; beat. Stir in eggs, sugar, juice, suet, and vanilla. In large bowl, combine flour with soda, salt, and spices. Add fruits and nuts. Mix well. Stir in bread mixture. Pour into well-greased 2-qt. mold. Cover with foil; tie with string. Place on metal rack or trivet in slow-cooking pot with 1 inch water. Cover pot and cook on high for 5 to 6 hours. Cool in pan 10 minutes; unmold. Serve warm, plain, or with hard sauce. Makes 10 to 12 servings.

CHOCOLATE PUDDING CAKE

2 cups flour
2 tsp. baking powder
¼ tsp. salt
½ cup cocoa powder
½ cup butter
½ cup sugar

4 eggs
1 cup milk
1½ cups fresh bread
  crumbs
Chocolate or fudge sauce

Grease 1½-qt. mold or baking dish. Sift flour, baking powder, salt, and cocoa. In large mixing bowl, cream butter and sugar; add eggs, one at a time, alternately with half the flour mixture. Beat well after each addition. Add milk alternately with remaining flour. Stir in bread crumbs. Pour into greased mold; cover with foil; tie. Place rack in slow-cooking pot. Add 2 cups hot water. Place mold with cake mixture on rack in pot. Cook, covered, on high for 3 to 4 hours. Serve warm or cold. To serve, slice cake and spoon chocolate or fudge topping over; top with whipped cream, if desired.

CARROT COFFEE CAKE

2 eggs
1 cup sugar
¾ cup salad oil
1½ cups flour
1 tsp. baking powder
¾ tsp. baking soda
⅛ tsp. salt
1 tsp. cinnamon
1 cup finely shredded
raw carrots

Beat eggs; add sugar gradually, beating until slightly thickened. Add oil gradually and continue beating until thoroughly combined. Stir in flour, baking powder, soda, salt, and cinnamon until mixture is smooth. Stir in carrots until blended well. Pour into greased and floured 6-cup mold. Cover with foil and tie. Put trivet or metal rack in slow-cooking pot. Pour 2 cups hot water in pot. Place filled mold on trivet or metal rack. Cover pot; cook on high for 2½ to 3½ hours or until done. Remove from pot; let stand 5 minutes on cooling rack. Loosen edges with knife. Turn out on rack and cool. This coffee cake can be used as a bread or cake. Serve either warm with butter, or cool with thin coating of butter or cream cheese frosting.

BANANA NUT CAKE

1 (18½-oz.) package
yellow cake mix
⅛ tsp. baking soda
1 cup water
2 eggs
1 cup mashed bananas
(2 medium bananas)
½ cup finely chopped
walnuts

In large mixing bowl, combine cake mix and soda. Add water, eggs, and bananas. Beat 4 minutes on medium speed of electric mixer. Fold in nuts. Pour into greased and floured 2-qt. mold. Place on bottom of slow-cooking pot. Cover cake with 4 to 5 paper towels. Cover pot and cook on high for 2 to 3 hours. Invert on cooling rack. Serve plain, dusted with powdered sugar, or drizzled with a thin glaze.

Short-Cut Fruit Cake
Courtesy California Raisin Advisory Board

SHORT-CUT FRUIT CAKE

1 (14-oz.) package date
  bar mix
⅔ cup hot water
3 eggs
¼ cup flour
¾ tsp. baking powder
2 tbs. light molasses

1 tsp. cinnamon
¼ tsp. nutmeg
¼ tsp. allspice
1 cup chopped nuts
1 cup raisins
1 (8-oz.) package candied
  red and green cherries

Grease and flour 6-cup ring mold. In large bowl, stir together date filling from date bar mix and water. Mix in dry crumbly mix, eggs, flour, baking powder, molasses, and spices thoroughly. Fold in nuts, raisins, and cherries. Spoon into mold. Cover with foil. Place metal rack or trivet in slow-cooking pot. Add 2 cups hot water.* Place filled mold in pot. Cover and cook on high for 2 to 3 hours. Cool and slice.

*Add more water after first hour of cooking, if needed.

APPLESAUCE SPICE CAKE

1 (1-lb. 3-oz.) package
spice cake mix

1 (1-lb.) can applesauce
2 eggs

Browned Butter Frosting:

⅓ cup butter
3 cups sifted powdered
sugar

1½ tsp. vanilla
2 tbs. milk

In large mixing bowl, combine cake mix with apple-sauce and eggs. Blend for ½ minute. Then beat at medium speed 4 minutes. Pour into greased and floured 6-cup mold. Place in slow-cooking pot. Arrange several layers of paper towels on top of mold. Cover slow-cooking pot, leaving lid slightly ajar. Cook on high for 2 to 3 hours. Let stand 5 minutes. Turn out on cooling rack. Cool; cover with frosting.

Frosting:

Heat butter in saucepan over medium heat until a delicate light brown, being careful not to let it get deep brown. Remove from heat. Stir in sugar, vanilla, and milk. Beat with a wooden spoon until smooth, adding a few drops of milk if mixture is too thick. Spread over cooled cake.

BLUEBERRY COFFEE CAKE

2 cups flour
1 cup sugar
4 tsp. baking powder
⅛ tsp. salt
2 eggs, beaten
½ cup salad oil

¼ cup milk
1 tsp. vanilla
2 cups fresh or thawed
  frozen blueberries,
  drained

Crumb Topping:
¼ cup softened butter
½ cup sugar

⅓ cup flour
½ tsp. ground cinnamon

In mixing bowl combine flour, sugar, baking powder and salt. Add eggs, oil, milk and vanilla. Beat until smooth. Fold in blueberries. Pour into greased 2-quart mold. Combine crumb topping ingredients and sprinkle on top of batter. Place in slow-cooking pot. Cover mold with 4 or 5 paper towels. Cover pot and cook on high 3 to 4 hours. Cool on rack for 5 minutes. Remove from mold. Serve warm. This dense blueberry coffee cake tastes great and would be ideal for Sunday brunch. Makes 6 to 8 servings.

FRUITS & DESSERTS

You can make desserts in your slow cooker. Actually, several types of desserts are perfectly suited because the slow cooker brings out those good old-fashioned flavors. It's hard to beat the taste of a fruit compote prepared in a pot. Long cooking at very low temperatures blends the fruit flavors with the spices, wines or liqueurs.

Fresh or dried fruits may be used in many combinations, depending on what's available in your market. Dried fruits are especially good when fixed in a slow cooker. Many of the desserts in this section are reminiscent of Grandmother's day. They require that old-time simmering which the slow cooker does so well.

If you have never tried real homemade mincemeat, try my *Mincemeat* recipe. It is a variation of an old Pennsylvania Dutch mince pie. Don't be frightened by the long list of ingredients. Cut the recipe in half if you want to start off on a smaller scale.

Traditional *Apple Butter* is so easy to make in a slow cooker. In the past you had to stir it almost constantly to keep it from sticking and scorching. That was before electrical slow cookers with low and even temperatures. And, you can "bake" custard in a slow cooker. With *Rice Pudding* or *Lemon Pudding* it is a good idea to turn the control to **HIGH**. The custardy mixture must be cooked on a trivet in hot water, so the trick is to cook it on **HIGH**.

Let me caution you that every baking container and mold will not fit all slow cookers. If you have a small cooker, you will have to use other molds or cut some of the recipes down to fit your pot. Measure your pot carefully, then take your tape measure with you when you shop for pans or molds.

APPLE PEANUT CRUMBLE

4 or 5 cooking apples,
  peeled and sliced
⅔ cup brown sugar,
  packed
½ cup flour
½ cup quick-cooking
  rolled oats

½ tsp. cinnamon
½ tsp. nutmeg
⅓ cup butter, softened
2 tbs. peanut butter

Place apple slices in slow-cooking pot. In medium
bowl, combine sugar, flour, oats, cinnamon, and nutmeg. Mix in butter and peanut butter with pastry
blender or fork. Sprinkle over apples. Cover pot and
cook on low for 5 to 6 hours. Serve warm; plain, with
ice cream or whipped cream. Makes 4 to 5 servings.

HOME-STYLE APPLESAUCE

8 to 10 medium cooking
  apples, peeled and
  diced

½ cup water
¾ cup sugar
Cinnamon

In slow-cooking pot, combine apples and water. Cover
and cook on low for 4 to 6 hours or until apples are
very soft. Add sugar and cook on low another 30 minutes. Sprinkle with cinnamon at serving time. Makes
about 4 cups.

Note: Applesauce will be slightly chunky. If smooth
sauce is preferred, puree or sieve cooked apples.

TRADITIONAL APPLE BUTTER

12 to 14 cooking apples   2 cups sugar
  (about 16 cups   1 tsp. ground cinnamon
  chopped)   ¼ tsp. ground cloves
2 cups cider

Core and chop apples. (Do not peel.) Combine apples
and cider in slow-cooking pot. Cover and cook on low
for 10 to 12 hours or until apples are mushy. Puree in
food mill or sieve. Return pureed mixture to pot; add
sugar, cinnamon, and cloves. Cover and cook on low
one hour. Will keep several weeks in the refrigerator.
Or, if desired, pour into hot sterilized jars and seal, or
pour into freezer containers and freeze. Makes about
8 cups.

FRESH PEARS IN WINE

6 small fresh pears   1 tsp. minced crystallized
1 cup sauterne wine   ginger
1 cup sugar   2 tbs. lemon juice
½ cup water

Peel pears, leaving fruit whole with stems intact. Place
upright in slow-cooking pot. Combine wine with sugar,
water, ginger, and lemon juice. Pour over pears. Cover
and cook on low 4 to 6 hours or until pears are tender.
Chill and serve plain, with sour cream or whipped
cream cheese. Makes 6 servings.

APPLE BROWN BETTY

4 cups small bread cubes
(about ½-inch)
½ cup melted butter or
margarine
½ tsp. ground cinnamon
¼ tsp. ground nutmeg

⅛ tsp. salt
¾ cup firmly packed
brown sugar
4 cups chopped, peeled
cooking apples

Mix bread cubes with butter, cinnamon, nutmeg, salt
and brown sugar. Arrange in alternate layers with
apples in slow-cooking pot. Cover and cook on high
for 1½ to 2½ hours or until apples are tender. Serve
warm with cream, hard sauce or ice cream. Makes 4
to 5 servings.

SPICY APPLESAUCE

8 to 10 medium apples
(eating kind)
½ cup water
¾ cup sugar

1 tsp. ground cinnamon
½ tsp. ground nutmeg
1 tsp. ground cloves

Cut apples into medium-size pieces; do not core or
peel. Place in slow-cooking pot with all other ingredients. Cook on low 7 to 8 hours until apples are very
soft. Strain through sieve. Serve hot or cold. Makes
about 4 cups.

BAKED APPLES

5 to 6 baking apples
½ cup raisins or chopped
  dates
1 cup brown sugar

1 cup boiling water
2 tbs. butter or margarine
½ tsp. ground cinnamon
¼ tsp. ground nutmeg

Core apples and peel each about ¼ way down. Arrange in slow-cooking pot. Fill centers with raisins or dates. Combine sugar, water, butter, cinnamon, and nutmeg. Pour over apples. Cover and cook on low 2 to 4 hours (depending on size and variety of apples). Serve warm or cool. Makes 5 to 6 servings.

DANISH APPLE PUDDING

1⅓ cups finely crushed
  zwieback (14 slices)
½ cup melted butter or
  margarine
½ cup brown sugar,
  packed

1 tsp. cinnamon
1 (16-oz.) can applesauce
½ cup chilled whipping
  cream

Combine zwieback crumbs with melted butter, sugar and cinnamon. Spoon applesauce into 1-qt. soufflé or baking dish. Top with crumb mixture. Place baking dish in slow-cooking pot. Cover pot and cook on low for 3 to 4 hours. Serve warm or chilled. Whip cream; spoon onto pudding. Makes 5 to 6 servings.

CARAMEL APPLES

2 (14-oz.) bags caramels   8 to 10 medium apples
¼ cup water

In slow-cooking pot, combine caramels and water.
Cover and cook on high for 1 to 1½ hours, stirring
frequently. Wash and dry apples. Insert stick into
stem end of each apple. Turn control on low. Dip
apple into hot caramel and turn to coat entire surface.
Holding apple above pot, scrape off excess accumula-
tion of caramel from bottom of apple. Place on greased
wax paper to cool.

SLOW-COOKING CRANBERRIES

1 (16-oz.) package fresh   2 cups sugar
   cranberries   ¼ cup water

Combine cranberries with sugar and water in slow-
cooking pot. Cover and cook on high 2 to 3 hours or
until some of the cranberries have "popped." Makes
about 4 cups. Serve with chicken or turkey.

ST. HELENA PEARS

6 fresh pears   ¼ cup brandy
½ cup raisins   ½ cup sauterne wine
¼ cup brown sugar   ½ cup macaroon crumbs
1 tsp. grated lemon peel

Peel and core pears; cut into thin slices. Mix raisins
with sugar and lemon peel. Arrange alternately with
pear slices in slow-cooking pot. Pour brandy and wine
over. Cover pot and cook on low for 4 to 6 hours.
Spoon into serving dishes, allow to cool. Sprinkle with
macaroons. Serve plain or topped with sour cream.
Makes 6 servings.

HOLIDAY FRUIT COMPOTE

¼ cup port wine
1 tbs. butter
1¼ cups sugar
1 tbs. grated lemon peel
⅛ tsp. cinnamon
⅛ tsp. nutmeg
4 medium apples, peeled
  and sliced

2 cups fresh cranberries
½ cup chopped pitted
  dates
⅓ cup chopped walnuts
Dairy sour cream or
  ice cream

In slow-cooking pot, combine wine, butter, sugar, lemon peel, and spices. Add apples and cranberries. Cover and cook on low for 4 to 6 hours. Stir in dates and walnuts. Serve warm or cold. Delicious with topping of sour cream or used as a sundae sauce for ice cream.

ORANGE-PRUNE COMPOTE

1 lb. dried prunes
3 cups water
2 (11-oz.) cans mandarin
  oranges, drained
⅓ cup sugar

¼ cup Cointreau or
  Curacao
½ cup orange juice
2 bananas, sliced

Pit prunes; combine with water in slow-cooking pot. Cover and cook on low for 2 to 2½ hours. Cool and drain. Combine with mandarin oranges, sugar, Cointreau, and orange juice. Let stand in refrigerator several hours. Just before serving, add bananas. Makes 8 to 10 servings.

APPLE-CRANBERRY COMPOTE

5 or 6 cooking apples,
  peeled and sliced
1 cup fresh cranberries
1 cup sugar

½ tsp. grated orange peel
½ cup water
¼ cup port wine
Dairy sour cream

Arrange apple slices and cranberries in slow-cooking pot. Sprinkle sugar over fruit. Add orange peel, water and wine. Stir to mix ingredients. Cover and cook on low for 4 to 6 hours or until apples are tender. Serve warm fruits with the juices, topped with dab of sour cream. Makes 5 to 6 servings.

STEAMED CHOCOLATE DESSERT

¼ cup butter or
  margarine
1⅛ cups sugar
1 egg, well beaten
1 cup fine dry bread
  crumbs
3 tbs. flour

1½ tsp. baking powder
¼ tsp. salt
½ cup milk
2 squares unsweetened
  chocolate, melted
½ tsp. vanilla
¼ cup chopped pecans

In large bowl, cream butter; add sugar gradually. Add eggs; mix until thick and fluffy. Combine dry bread crumbs, flour, baking powder and salt. Add milk, alternately with dry ingredients, to sugar-butter mixture beginning and ending with dry ingredients. Stir in melted chocolate, vanilla and pecans. Pour into greased 1-quart mold. Cover with foil; tie. Place on metal rack or trivet in slow-cooking pot. Pour 2 cups hot water around mold. Cover pot; cook on high for 2 to 3 hours. Spoon into bowls and serve with whipped cream or mint ice cream. Makes 4 to 6 servings.

CROCKERY-STEWED PRUNES

1 (1-lb.) package dried
  prunes

3 cups water
2 thin lemon slices

In slow-cooking pot, combine prunes with water and
lemon slices. Cover and cook on low for 2 hours or
until prunes are plump and tender. Serve warm or
cold. Makes 6 to 8 servings.

FRUIT MEDLEY

1½ lbs. mixed dried
  fruits
2½ cups water
1 cup sugar
1 tbs. honey
Peel of ½ lemon, cut into
  thin strips

⅛ tsp. nutmeg
1 cinnamon stick
3 tbs. cornstarch
¼ cup Cointreau

Put dried fruit into slow-cooking pot. Pour in water.
Stir in sugar, honey, lemon peel, and spices. Cover and
cook on low for 2 to 3 hours. Turn control to high. Mix
cornstarch in small amount of water; stir into fruit
mixture. Cook on high for 10 minutes or until thickened. Add Cointreau. Serve warm or chilled. May be
served as fruit compote or as topping for ice cream.
Makes 5 to 6 servings.

HOMEMADE MINCEMEAT

2½ lbs. beef shanks
4 cups water
½ lb. beef suet
2 lbs. tart apples, peeled and diced
1 (15-oz.) package seedless raisins
1 (11-oz.) package currants
1 tbs. grated lemon peel
1 tbs. lemon juice

1 tbs. grated orange peel
¼ cup orange juice
1 tsp. cinnamon
½ tsp. ground cloves
½ tsp. nutmeg
1 tsp. salt
½ cup molasses
½ cup brown sugar, packed
1½ cups apple cider

Combine beef and water in slow-cooking pot. Cover and cook on low for 8 to 10 hours. Save all the broth; remove beef from bones. In food chopper, grind beef and suet together. Combine with ½ cup broth and remaining ingredients in slow-cooking pot. Cover and cook on low 8 to 10 hours. Makes 3 qts. mincemeat or enough for four 9-inch pies. In making pies, 2 or 3 tbs. brandy or bourbon may be added to filling for each pie. Filling can be kept in refrigerator for several days or frozen for about 6 months. Extra broth can be used for soup base.

DOWN-HOME RHUBARB

2 lbs. fresh rhubarb (about 7 to 8 cups)
½ cup water

1½ cups sugar
½ tsp. vanilla (optional)

Trim rhubarb and cut into 1-inch pieces. Combine with water and sugar in slow-cooking pot. Cover and cook on low 2 to 3 hours. Add vanilla, if desired. Chill. Makes about 4 cups.

SPICED RHUBARB BAKE

1½ lbs. fresh rhubarb
¾ cup sugar
1 cinnamon stick
3 whole cloves
1 tsp. grated orange or
  lemon peel

¼ cup butter or
  margarine
¼ cup flour
⅓ cup sugar

Cut rhubarb into 1-inch pieces. In slow-cooking pot, combine rhubarb with ¾ cup sugar, cinnamon, cloves, and grated peel. Cover and cook on low for 3 to 4 hours. Remove cinnamon and cloves. Spoon rhubarb into shallow baking dish. In small bowl, mix together butter, flour and ⅓ cup sugar with fork or pastry blender. Sprinkle over cooked rhubarb. Bake in 400°F. oven for about 20 minutes. Makes 5 to 6 servings.

LEMON PUDDING CAKE

3 eggs, separated
1 tsp. grated lemon peel
¼ cup lemon juice
3 tbs. butter

1½ cups milk
¾ cup sugar
¼ cup flour
⅛ tsp. salt

Beat egg whites until stiff peaks form; set aside. Beat egg yolks; blend in lemon peel, juice, butter, and milk. Combine sugar, flour, and salt; add to egg-milk mixture, beating until smooth. Fold into beaten whites. Spoon into slow-cooking pot. Cover and cook on high for 2 to 3 hours. Makes 5 to 6 servings.

HOME-STYLE BREAD PUDDING

2 eggs, slightly beaten
2¼ cups milk
1 tsp. vanilla
½ tsp. ground cinnamon
¼ tsp. salt

2 cups 1-inch bread
cubes
½ cup brown sugar
½ cup raisins or
chopped dates

In medium mixing bowl, combine eggs with milk, vanilla, cinnamon, salt, bread, sugar, and raisins or dates. Pour into 1½-qt. baking dish. Place metal trivet or rack in bottom of slow-cooking pot. Add ½ cup hot water. Set baking dish on trivet. Cover pot; cook on high for about 2 hours. Serve pudding warm or cool. Makes 4 to 6 servings.

RICE PUDDING

1 cup uncooked regular
rice
3 cups milk
3 tbs. butter
½ tsp. salt

½ cup sugar
3 eggs, beaten
1 tsp. vanilla
1 cup raisins
Cinnamon

Cook rice according to package directions. Combine cooked rice with milk, butter, salt, sugar, eggs, vanilla, and raisins. Pour into 1½-qt. baking dish. Sprinkle with cinnamon. Cover baking dish with foil, not plastic. Place on metal trivet or rack in bottom of slow-cooking pot. Add 1 cup hot water to pot. Cover and cook on high for 2 hours. Makes 6 to 8 servings.

FAVORITE BAKED CUSTARD

2 cups milk, scalded   1 tsp. vanilla
3 eggs, slightly beaten   ⅛ tsp. salt
⅓ cup sugar   Nutmeg or coconut

Scald milk, let cool slightly. Combine eggs, sugar,
vanilla, and salt. Slowly stir in slightly cooled milk.
Pour into buttered 1-qt. baking dish. Sprinkle with
nutmeg or coconut. Cover with foil. Set baking dish
on metal rack or trivet in slow-cooking pot. Pour hot
water around baking dish, 1 inch deep. Cover pot and
cook on high for 2 to 2½ hours or until knife inserted
in custard comes out clean. Serve warm or chilled.
Makes 5 to 6 servings.

CHOCOLATE FONDUE

6 (1-oz.) squares   Angel cake cut into
  unsweetened chocolate   bite-size chunks
1½ cups sugar   Marshmallows
1 cup light cream   Fruits (such as bananas,
½ cup butter or   strawberries,
  margarine   maraschino cherries,
⅛ tsp. salt   or pineapple)
3 tbs. creme de cacao or
  coffee-flavored liqueur

Place chocolate in slow-cooking pot. Cover and heat
on high for about 30 minutes or until chocolate melts.
Stir in sugar, cream, butter, and salt. Cook on high,
stirring constantly, for about 10 minutes or until
blended. Add creme de cacao. Turn control to low.
Spear angel cake chunks, marshmallows or fruits with
fondue fork. Dip into chocolate mixture. Keep chocolate hot in slow-cooking pot. Makes about 6 to 8
servings.

MINT WAFERS

2 tbs. butter
¼ cup milk
1 package (about 15 oz.) white creamy frosting mix

Several drops mint flavoring
Food coloring (optional)

Combine butter and milk in slow-cooking pot. Turn control to high; cover and heat until butter melts. Stir in frosting mix. Cook on high for 1 to 2 minutes, stirring occasionally. Add flavoring and color, if desired. Turn to low. Drop from teaspoon onto waxed paper, swirling tips with spoon. Keep slow-cooking pot control on low while forming patties. If candy gets too thick, add several drops hot water. Makes 5 dozen.

MILK CHOCOLATE SAUCE

1 (16-oz.) milk chocolate candy bar
1 cup light cream

⅓ cup butter
1 tsp. vanilla

In slow-cooking pot, break chocolate into small pieces. Add cream and butter. Cover and cook on low for 2 to 2½ hours or until chocolate melts. Stir in vanilla. Beat until smooth. Serve warm over pound cake, angel cake, or ice cream. Makes about 3 cups sauce.

ROSY FRUIT TOPPING

1 (20-oz.) can pineapple chunks
1 (29-oz.) can sliced cling peaches
3 tbs. butter

½ cup currant jelly
1 tsp. grated lemon peel
½ cup peach brandy, heated
Vanilla ice cream

Drain pineapple and peaches. Combine fruit with butter, jelly, and lemon peel in slow-cooking pot. Cover and cook on low for 2 to 3 hours. Stir in warm brandy. Spoon over ice cream. Makes 8 servings.

INDEX

SPICE CHART

NAME AND DESCRIPTION	COMPATIBLE WITH:
Allspice Color—brown Flavor—spicy, sweet, mild, pleasant	All cranberry dishes, spice cakes, beef stew, baked ham, mincemeat and pumpkin pie, tapioca & chocolate pudding
Anise Color—brown with tan stripes Flavor—sweet licorice aroma and taste	Coffee cake, rolls, cookies, all fruit pie fillings, sweet pickles, stewed fruits
Basil Color—light green Flavor—mild, sweet	All tomato dishes, green vegetables, stews, shrimp and lobster dishes
Bay Leaves Color—light green Flavor—very mild, sweet	Vegetables, stews, shrimp lobster, chicken dishes, pot roasts
Caraway Color—dark brown with light brown stripes Flavor—like rye bread	Cheese spreads, breads and rolls, cookies, vegetables, roast pork
Cardamom Color—cream-colored pod, dark brown seeds Flavor—bitter-sweet	Danish pastry, coffee cake, custards, sweet potato and pumpkin dishes
Cayenne Color—burnt orange Flavor—hot	Deviled eggs, fish dishes, cooked green vegetables, cheese soufflés, pork chops, veal stew
Celery Seed Color—shades of brownish green Flavor—bitter celery	Meat loaf, fish chowders, cole slaw, stewed tomatoes, rolls, salad dressings
Chili Powder Color—light to dark red Flavor—distinctive, hot	Mexican cookery, chili, beef, pork and veal dishes, Spanish rice
Cinnamon Color—light brown Flavor—sweet and spicy	Coffee cakes, spice cake, cookies, puddings, fruit pies, spiced beverages, sweet potato and pumpkin dishes

NAME AND DESCRIPTION

COMPATIBLE WITH:

Cloves
Color—dark brown
Flavor—spicy, sweet, pungent

Ham, apple, mince & pumpkin pies, baked beans, hot tea, spice cake, puddings, cream of pea and tomato soups

Cumin
Color—gold with a hint of green
Flavor—salty sweet

Deviled eggs, chili, rice, fish

Curry Powder
Color—predominantly rich gold
Flavor—exotic with heat

Eggs, fish, poultry, creamed vegetables, chowders, tomato soup, salted nuts

Dill
Color—greenish brown
Flavor—similar to caraway, but milder and sweeter

Pickling, potato salad, soups, vegetables, salad dressing, drawn butter for shellfish

Ginger
Color—tan
Flavor—spicy

Cookies, spice cake, pumpkin pie, puddings, applesauce, stews, French dressing

Mace
Color—burnt orange
Flavor—similar to nutmeg, exotic

Fish, stews, pickling, gingerbread, cakes. Welsh rarebit, chocolate dishes, fruit pies

Marjoram
Color—green
Flavor—delicate

Lamb chops, roast beef, poultry, omelets, stews, stuffings

Mint
Color—green
Flavor—sweet

Jelly, fruit salad, lamb and veal roast, tea

Mustard
Color—light to dark brown
Flavor—spicy, sharp

Pickling, Chinese hot sauce, cheese sauce, vegetables, molasses cookies

Nutmeg
Color—copper
Flavor—exotic, sweet

Doughnuts, eggnog, custards, spice cake, coffee cake, pumpkin pie, sweet potatoes

Oregano
Color—green
Flavor—strong

Pizza, spaghetti sauce, meat sauces, soups, vegetables

NAME AND DESCRIPTION

COMPATIBLE WITH:

Paprika
Color—red
Flavor—very mild

Poultry, goulash, vegetables, canapes, chowders

Parsley
Color—green
Flavor—mild

Soups, salads, meat stews, all vegetables, potatoes

Pepper
Color—black or white
Flavor—spicy, enduring aftertaste

Almost all foods except those with sweet flavors. Use white pepper when black specks are not desired.

Poppy Seeds
Color—blue-gray
Flavor—crunchy, nutlike

Breads and rolls, salad dressings, green peas

Rosemary
Color—green
Flavor—delicate, sweetish

Lamb, beef, pork, poultry, soups, cheese sauces, potatoes

Saffron
Color—red-orange
Flavor—exotic

Rice, breads, fish stew, chicken soup, cakes

Savory
Color—green
Flavor—mild, pleasant

Scrambled eggs, poultry stuffing, hamburgers, fish, tossed salad

Sesame Seeds
Color—cream
Flavor—crunchy, nutlike

Breads and rolls, cookies, salad dressings, fish, asparagus

Tarragon
Color—green
Flavor—fresh, pleasant

Marinades of meat, poultry, omelets, fish, soups, vegetables

Thyme
Color—olive green
Flavor—pleasantly penetrating

Tomato dishes, fish chowder, all meats, potatoes

Tumeric
Color—orange
Flavor—mild, slightly bitter

Pickles, salad dressings, seafood, rice